MY DAUGHTER'S STRUGGLE WITH EPILEPSY
AND HER BOUNDLESS WILL TO LIVE

SHE
DANCED
WITH
LIGHTNING

MARC PALMIERI

POST Hill
PRESS

A POST HILL PRESS BOOK
ISBN: 978-1-63758-420-0
ISBN (eBook): 978-1-63758-421-7

She Danced with Lightning:
My Daughter's Struggle with Epilepsy and Her Boundless Will to Live
© 2022 by Marc Palmieri
All Rights Reserved

Post Hill Press
New York • Nashville
posthillpress.com

Published in the United States of America
1 2 3 4 5 6 7 8 9 10

Once up, once down the hill, one journey, Babe,
That will suffice thee; and it seems that now
Thou hast fore-knowledge that such task is thine;
Thou travell'st so contently, and sleep'st
In such a heedless peace. Alas!

—William Wordsworth, *To My Infant Daughter*

For the grandparents: Bruce, Frank, Geri, Maureen

TABLE OF CONTENTS

PROLOGUE

The article in the *New York Daily News* was set to appear in print on June 18. That morning, while the girls dressed for school, I drove to the Wan Wan Mart, a deli a few blocks from us. I parked, ran inside, and saw the fresh morning papers near the cash register. I flipped through one and found the story about my daughter's epilepsy.

I realized that this morning, June 18, marked exactly one year since Anna's brain surgery. A coincidence.

"You want to buy it?" the deli man said.

"I'll take five."

"Five *Daily News*?"

"About my daughter," I said, holding up the page.

He squinted and read a bit.

"God bless," he said. "Take for free."

I thanked him but paid anyway.

A sixty-dollar parking ticket was on my windshield. You can't park on that side of the street after 7 a.m. The ticket read 7:06 a.m. In New York City, there is supposed to be a five-minute grace period for parking tickets. If so, I was one minute over. The traffic cop must have been standing there waiting, I thought, staring at his watch. I looked around. Not a traffic cop in sight. Considering the story in the papers under my arm, a story in tabloid black and white about how my child had been saved, I laughed. The first funny parking ticket in my life.

Not that it was funny to lose money. We didn't have a lot to waste, and we'd been trying hard to save. We'd soon be taking our annual road trip to see my brother Scott's family in Rhode Island and no doubt spend twice what we intended. Our daughters loved to be with their cousins, and we'd come to call our few nights together "Happy Fourth" (pronounced with an exaggerated New England accent), a little Independence Day tradition now running as long as we had children.

In a few weeks, we drove up and had a terrific time as always, every now and then stopping to appreciate how much had changed in just one year. Last Happy Fourth, my very swollen-faced, nauseous, and drugged-up twelve-year-old wore a headscarf to cover the stitches along the still-fresh scar that ran over her scalp. Now, she was swimming with her cousins in the Atlantic.

We arrived home in Queens late that Sunday. As Kristen and I unpacked our bags in the living room, Nora, our ten-year-old, called me upstairs. When Anna started middle school the year before, we got her a smartphone. We hadn't planned on Nora getting one yet but caved pretty fast at her argument of birth-order discrimination.

When I got to her room, she was sitting on her bed.

"Daddy, I want you to see this but not really," Nora said, looking at her phone. It was a headline from TMZ. A friend had sent it to her.

CAMERON BOYCE, DISNEY ACTOR, DEAD AT 20

I'd seen this kid on our television a thousand times. *Jessie, The Descendants*.... I remembered one day, Anna was complaining about having freckles, and I used Boyce as an example of someone with freckles who was very successful, talented, and happy.

"I read it," Nora said. "He had a seizure."

Then came the familiar, abrupt gear shifts within me. My circulation working at its max, I started reading the article. The family confirmed he had epilepsy and had died in bed.

In the days that followed, we saw news reports about Boyce's death, many trying to explain epilepsy to the viewing public. Guest medical experts showed digital graphics of how brains were electrocuted by malfunctioning nerve cells leaking charges. Stories came on about seizure dogs, medications, and SUDEP, an acronym that had haunted us since Anna was five months old. It stands for "Sudden Unexpected Death in Epilepsy." It's what kills one in one thousand people with epilepsy every year, the reason they are twenty-four times more likely to die suddenly than the general population. Most often, SUDEP happens during sleep.

"Is that what could have happened to Anna?" Nora said when I handed her phone back.

"Yes," I said.

"Daddy?"

"Yes, Nora."

"All that stuff, will it ever happen again?"

I don't think I answered her. I should have said, "No, never. Anna is okay, Nora. Didn't you see the *Daily News* feature, framed and hanging in her room? It's been over a year already. So many things are easier now, so many things are better. For all of us."

But I didn't.

"It's late," I said. "You guys are up early tomorrow. Let's get to sleep."

The girls were starting their summer day camps the next morning. We said goodnight, and I flipped Nora's light out on the way into the hall, where I went and stood outside Anna's bedroom door.

"Goodnight, Anna," I said.

"Goodnight, Daddy," she said from within.

I turned to head back down to finish unpacking but stopped when I got to the top of the stairs. I remembered Nora standing there one afternoon, on the first step down the steep wooden decline. She was holding onto her big sister, her arms wrapped around her. Anna had seized, and Nora made it to her just in time.

I turned back and lay down on the floor outside Anna's room. I rested my head on my hands, keeping my ear as close to the space under the door as I could.

Monday morning came. Anna had slept soundly. I'd slept an hour, maybe two.

CHAPTER ONE

IT WAS SPRING

We were finally outside on a ball field.

For a former baseball player, there's nothing like the first warm day. March of this year had been all snow, rain, and wicked wind. Long ago, I left New York and went down south to play, and it was a great thing to have baseball weather in February. When my playing days were over, I returned. A month like the one we'd just had could have me thinking about going back to warmer climates, but in New York City, there were so many neurologists, hospitals, and emergency rooms. I knew we'd never leave.

Spring was finally taking hold on this April Saturday, with a sun that seemed like it was borrowed from mid-May. Anna had a softball game. As we pulled into the field's parking lot, I could see the grass was dry, and there wasn't the slightest puddle on the infield. I then noticed that this place, somewhere off the Belt Parkway in Rockaway, had an outdoor batting cage. Nobody was using it. We were a few minutes early, so I told Anna to hurry her cleats on so she could take some warm-up swings.

I wasn't the coach, but I'd help out when I could be at practices or games. This was rare. I taught most weekday afternoons into evenings and had a side job coaching travel baseball. As it was, I could barely fit in time to write and go on the occasional acting audition. Nothing new for me. Ever since I decided to try to get into theatre some twenty-five years earlier, I'd been far more successful accumulating "day jobs."

Anna was pulling the first cleat onto her foot, and of course, she didn't bother untying it first. I yelled at her to hurry up. We'd recently raised her medication dose, and for a moment, I wondered if her sluggishness this morning was related to that. But then again, she'd been sluggish in the morning all her life. She had a nice peaceful sleep the night before, as far as I could remember. Sometimes, in the morning, it took a few hours for me to recall exactly what had gone on through the night, sort of like the way one might remember a dream late the next day or never remember it at all. Same with the nights of Anna's seizures.

My father was with us. He'd come early to Queens to pick us up, bringing egg sandwiches from a deli near where he and my mother lived on Long Island. Anna was always a gourmand for comfort food: burgers, fries, pancakes, pizza, bagels, egg sandwiches…. Still, she was lean and strong, and by the hundreds of blood tests she'd taken in her near twelve-year life, we knew, besides the heavy medicine levels, she had nice, healthy chemistry. The new med she was on, Lacosamide, was the seventh we were trying since her diagnosis. She was also taking medical marijuana.

My father had been saying he wanted to come to Anna's games as soon as the weather allowed one to actually be played, and finally, here we were. While I unzipped Anna's bat bag, I noticed he was on a knee, helping her with her second cleat. I grabbed a ball and bat and jogged to the batting cage.

The year Anna was born, I'd started a part time job in Harlem as an adjunct lecturer at The City College of New York.

Two months into my first semester there, teaching an undergraduate playwriting class, we learned she had epilepsy. It was on a November morning. I was wearing a corduroy blazer I'd bought to wear at my new job on campus, looking, I imagined, how I'd always pictured myself looking if someday I had made it as a playwright with a job teaching at a famous college. I was on my walk to the subway, down the long hill from Amsterdam to Broadway, when my flip phone vibrated. It was Kristen, my wife. I answered and was about to tell her that I'd just spoken, I believed, with reasonable accuracy to my students about a certain Shakespeare play. Maybe I was about to tell her how happy it had made me.

"We're on the way to the hospital," she said, tense but calm. "Anna's having seizures."

I'd only seen one seizure in my whole life. It was a girl who sat next to me in seventh-grade Home Economics class. She leaned over, fell out of her desk, shaking with spittle bubbling in the corners of her lips. I can still see the frightful face she made, as if she was taking punches she couldn't block. The teacher ran to her, calling her name. Others came in and carried her out of the room. Some kids laughed.

I asked Kristen where the hospital was.

"68th and York. Please meet me there."

Anna had just turned five months old and was twenty-four inches long—exactly the length of a pitcher's mound rubber. We'd learn later that she was suffering a "cluster" of what they called partial complex seizures. Her eyes would avert, and her lips smacked as her right arm rose and stiffened. Her breath would seem to labor. She'd snap back to consciousness for a moment, smile, as if just discovering her parents there, hovering over her, then the next seizure would start. Before the doctors were able to stop them, Anna had forty of these ninety-second attacks, and reached a near "status epilepticus," which means there was virtually no time between them—a state of near permanent seizure, a spiral toward escalating brain damage and death.

From inside the batting cage, I watched Anna walk toward me. She still seemed groggy, but I wasn't alarmed. Not yet. She wasn't used to morning sports. If this were a dance event, she'd be different. Dance had always been Anna's first love. She played Little League sports—soccer, softball, volleyball—but it was dancing she'd rather wake up early for. Same with Nora. Our little house in Bayside, with its original battered wooden floors from 1930, could sound like a bustling midtown tap studio, or a hip-hop concert, morning to night.

I told Anna to hurry again. She trotted toward me.

"That's it!" I said. "Now, you're lookin' like a ballplayer!"

She did. Shiny cleats, black baseball pants, and a bright red jersey tucked in tight. It had been ten whole nights without a seizure, which was the longest she'd gone in two years. Or maybe even two and a half. We used to keep a calendar, but at some point, the record-keeping felt like a waste of time. I gave my throwing arm a quick stretch. It was stiff as hell, and I felt a tightness in my neck and upper back. Nothing new. I slept on a floor every night, after all.

We had the house now, but beforehand, Kristen and I had lived in apartments, and our last place had wood floors too. Hardwood looks nice and works great for practicing tap and jazz steps, but it's no place to get a comfortable rest. For the last couple years, I'd spent my nights on it, right beside Anna's bed. Air mattresses take too much time to set up, make too much noise, and usually deflate through the night under guys my size.

Instead, I'd lay down thick blankets to make the floor soft enough that I wouldn't feel the stiffness and bone aching until morning.

There was no choice about all this. Since she was three, all her seizures came during sleep, and when they did, she had to be protected. Her arms would contract and her clenched fists pulled inward with a titan's might. Even I, at over two hundred pounds, needed all my mettle to keep them from crushing her nose and throat. And then, there was the writhing and kicking. Kristen and I took turns in the bed for the earlier years, but by now, Anna, at eleven, was nearly Kristen's size, and so it had to be me, and we felt it better at this age that she sleep in her own bed in her own room, so her floor would be for me.

My sleep was a paradox. I slept, but with full awareness. I would snap awake with every slight shift of Anna's body, twitch of a limb, or change in breathing pattern. I'd shoot up, grab the flashlight I kept next to my head and check if her eyes were open, which they'd be, wild and wide, if a seizure was starting. I'd clamber up and position my legs over hers, then get my arms between her face and fists, then hold, count, and wait. I would put my cheek on her head and tell her I was there, and after a couple minutes, it would be over. We'd both be asleep again. It took a number of these nocturnal seizures, maybe a thousand or so, before I mastered my approach, safely positioning my weight correctly. Even with experience, it could still get rough. Once, she hit her forehead on the wall so hard that her large, baroquely framed painting of a ballet dancer fell off the wall and crashed on my head. Another night, when I hadn't noticed she'd turned her body halfway around before I got to her, she broke my nose with her heel. Anna once joked I should wear catcher's equipment to sleep.

Anna was in the cage, taking her stance in the dirt patch of a batter's box. I tried the underhand fastpitch, since that's what she'd see in the game, but I wasn't even close. My pitch was at her ankles and barely crossed the plate without bouncing. She swung anyway, level and aggressive. The hips rotated, her wrists turned over nicely, and she kept her head down. It was a damn good-looking swing, but the ball had rolled into the net behind her. Bad pitch, I said apologetically.

When I was eighteen, I was drafted as a pitcher by the Toronto Blue Jays, offered a minor league contract, and assigned to their Pioneer League team in Alberta, where it was even colder than Queens in March. Even in my forties, I liked to think I could still bring the heat pretty good, but as for softball's windmill underhand stuff, I was useless.

"Get the ball, Anna."

She was still standing in the batter's box.

"The ball, Anna. Go get it."

I checked the time on my phone and looked toward the parking lot. I saw a few more red jerseys. Her team was arriving. I turned back around. She hadn't moved.

"Anna, would you please get the ball?"

She dropped the bat, staring at me.

"We only have a minute here!" I said.

"Daddy?"

She ran to me, hard. My first thought was that she'd seen someone she didn't like and was taking cover. These were middle school days now, so anything was possible.

"What's wrong?"

She threw her arms around me and squeezed, making rhythmic gasps for air. Her left leg rose and wrapped itself behind my calf. She began to droop, hanging on to my arms. She's awake, I thought. It's daytime. So this can't be a seizure.

"Daddy..." she said.

It was a strange quirk of Anna's frontal-lobe epilepsy that the ravage would only happen during sleep. By day, though beaten to hell by the heavy meds and sleep deprivation, Anna would rise, get to school, dance, have friends, and appear to most, even herself, even to us, as having a normal childhood, just one with blood tests every three months, a parent on her floor at night, exhaustion, and no sleepovers. We felt that hers was an oddly fortunate version of this horrible disorder. Some nights, she could have seven or eight seizures across as many hours, and we couldn't imagine that being the case by day. Strange to both hate this thing yet dread that it might ever change.

"Sharks," she said.

"What?"

"Sharks are coming at me."

"Sharks?"

I turned and looked around. For what, I didn't know. Maybe for sharks. I held her up in front of me.

"Are you feeling like you're having a seizure?"

It was a pointless question. Anna wouldn't know what seizures felt like. She'd never remember anything if I asked about them in the morning. I looked into her eyes. She was looking right at me. They weren't averting, but her right hand dropped, brushing my arm. I looked at it. It was limp. I grabbed it.

"Make a fist," I said.

She couldn't.

Then, I remembered something. The week prior, she was in the living room, having just gotten up for school. Kristen had already left for work. Nora was in the shower. I'd gone outside to take in the garbage cans, and when I came back inside, Anna was crying.

"What's the matter?" I said at the time.

"My legs," she sobbed. "They felt heavy."

"What do you mean?"

"I came downstairs, and they just felt heavy."

I said her legs had gone to sleep, that's all.

"Did you sit on the toilet too long after you woke up?" I said. "If you sit too long, that can happen."

"Maybe."

"And all is normal now?"

"Yeah."

"Then don't worry! That's all it was."

And just like that, I'd dismissed it, and since then, there had been nothing out of the norm. We were up to ten nights of peace. Or maybe, I recalculated quickly, tonight would make the tenth. So it was nine. Still a long stretch. It had to be at least nine, I then thought. But even eight would be encouraging. Was it eight? Maybe tonight would make nine....

Anna reached for her chest and pulled at her jersey. Her eyes darted left, then rolled back. Her lips turned blue, and she collapsed. As her head hit my chest, I remembered something else, clear as day. There was a seizure. Sometime last night, deep in the night. It was on the shorter side maybe, or maybe I caught it only halfway through. But there was a seizure last night for sure.

"Hospital," my father said. "Right now." He already had her bat and bag. I lifted Anna up and ran toward the parking lot. Red jerseys passed by in my periphery.

"Marc?" one of them said.

It was head coach Ari. She was carrying the team helmet bag, holding her clipboard, looking at me as I approached, and nodding, sadly. I looked in her eyes. It seemed they were asking me questions, the questions I was asking myself: "Is this is it, Marc? Is the scene finally here? The one you knew would come someday? The one you can't survive? The one you don't *want* to survive?"

Nearly a dozen years of it. Half awake, dragged forward by delusions and denial. Pharmaceuticals. Ketogenic diet. Gluten-free diet. Marijuana pills. Fish oil pills. Melatonin pills. Coconut oil. Prayers. Nothing would ever work. It wanted her dead. It's what it wanted since that November afternoon, when she was the length of a pitching rubber, and I wore a corduroy blazer and still slept in a bed. Anyone who knew us had to know this scene would come someday. It's what makes tragedy so moving in the theatre—*Oedipus, Romeo and Juliet, Cyrano*...name it... everyone knows the ending is unbearable, but somehow, even as the story rolls headlong toward it, the audience thinks maybe, just maybe, this time, it'll be different. It's part of what they call "suspension of disbelief." It's a useful human ability. It gets you through until the ending.

Despite my best efforts to avoid thinking about it, how our life with Anna was so much more likely than most to come to an early end, I couldn't always resist. I'd picture the final scene playing out in countless ways and places. I would see it most every night really, my cheek on her head, the silent, inner storm stealing her from the world for ninety long seconds. I'd whisper that I was there, waiting for her to come back, holding her, and that I loved her, that someday, this would end, one way or another. It had to.

I'd see it, the ending, there in her room, at school, on the street, in the car, at a party, at dance class, or face down one morning in her bed above mine, dead of SUDEP. I saw it in so many ways, but I hadn't seen it like this, at a ball field, on the first beautiful day of a long-awaited spring.

*

We were crawling on the parkway, but in a strange way, I was glad, since I wasn't sure where we were actually going. I rushed out an email to Anna's neurologist, which was the best way of getting a message to her on a weekend. I also sent a text message to my aunt Maureen, a physician's assistant and my family's personal hotline for all things medical. I held off calling Kristen. I wanted to keep my attention on Anna and not risk any calls from my aunt or the doctor going to voicemail.

Her neurologist was with NYU, and the question was whether we should drive all the way there to the east side of Manhattan. I thought of locating whatever hospital was closest by typing "hospital" into the maps app on my phone, but I couldn't bring my fingers to do it—I had barely gotten the email and text spelled out without dropping the phone to the floor. My father didn't say much, but after passing an exit or two, as we started to pick up speed, he asked what I wanted to do once we reached the other parkways. Just east, there were hospitals not far from where we live, but I thought it might be best to get to where her doctors and records were. My father agreed. When we got to the exit, we'd head west for the Midtown Tunnel.

Anna looked like she was having a heart attack. This wasn't an impossibility. When her seizures came at night, her heart would race, and there would come a moment, right as the stiffness and kicking eased, when her entire body would loosen, as if lifeless. It seemed to me that the heart would stop—ribcage silent, switched off for a few seconds before it restarted, and the seizure was over. To try to confirm this, I once bought a stethoscope at CVS and,

SHE DANCED WITH LIGHTNING

for a while, slept with it around my neck, thinking I would pop it in my ears when a seizure hit, hold her, push the diaphragm piece against her chest, and listen. That endeavor didn't last long. She made too much noise grunting and shuffling for me to hear clearly or even land the piece flat on her skin. I must have looked ridiculous wresting with her, taking blows to the face and chest, while leaning in with the stethoscope. The thing ended up in a toybox in the basement.

I kept talking to Anna, who had now regained full consciousness. I asked her what she felt, which seemed to be in flux—as if something painful was coursing through her, across her—first, she would say her fingers hurt, then her palms, then her arms, then her chest. When the sensation would roll up her torso, she became more agitated and fearful. Then, it would drain away. She looked pale, her lips dry, still off-color. Nothing here looked like any seizures we'd ever seen. I asked her to try to lift her left arm. She did it, but slowly. She then effortfully pushed both arms up and out, letting her hands weakly float in the air. Her index fingers and pinkies elongated.

"What are you doing?" I asked.

"Ballet hands," she said. "I can make them, but they're so heavy."

She brought both down to her sides.

"I have floppy arms," she said. "I can't have floppy arms tonight."

I didn't yet realize what she'd meant about "tonight." I would have asked, but my phone rang. Aunt Maureen.

"What's happening with Anna?" she said, with a veteran medic's focus. I tried to explain what I saw at the field and what I was seeing in the car. I told her I was wondering whether we should head all the way into Manhattan or—

"The nearest ER," she said. "Where are you?"

She told us where to go. There was a hospital a few miles away. My father started to speed. My aunt asked me to describe the symptoms again, then told me exactly what to say to the doctors when we got to the ER. She told me she loved me, and to keep her posted. Then, I called Kristen. She answered the phone with a happy Saturday morning voice. She told me she'd just dropped Nora at the dance studio for class, then asked me how the softball game was going.

We pulled up to the ER entrance. I helped Anna out of the car, and my father pulled away to park. She had regained a bit of breath and was able to walk now, wobbly, leaning on me. The receiving area was partitioned into cubicles with glass walls. We were led to a tiny workspace and asked a series of basic questions. As Anna, in her softball uniform, described what she felt at the field and in the car, it occurred to me that anyone who saw us here would think she twisted an ankle or strained a muscle.

We'd done ERs many times, so I don't know why I would expect more of a sense of haste here, but I did. It was as if I thought the whole medical world should already know Anna's seizures never came like this, during the day, and that this could be a devastating game changer, so of course we'd skip the irritating routine of the admitting procedure. It felt like we should already be racing Anna down a hallway on a gurney, doctors and nurses barking vitals, holding an oxygen mask to her face, as I jogged alongside, telling her all would be okay as they disappeared through double doors, an orderly blocking me from proceeding, saying something like, "Sir, your daughter's in good hands now." I was outwardly calm, but everything inside me, standing there, felt as if it were in hysteria—my heart, my thoughts, my blood—as an expressionless receiving nurse checked boxes on her clipboard in no apparent rush at all.

My father came in. I told the nurse I thought a doctor should see Anna right away. She didn't respond but leaned down and reached for something printing under her desk. When she sat back up, I saw it was the ID band for Anna's wrist. The nurse fastened it on, and behind me appeared a muscular, tattooed technician with a wheelchair. Things were moving faster than I'd thought. The tech and my father helped Anna into the chair and took her away. I was asked to sign papers and present insurance information. I reached for my wallet.

I could have been wrong, but I was fairly sure we hadn't been to this particular hospital before, but we were already in their computer system. They had my elapsed Screen Actors Guild insurance information and an outdated home address. It'd been a few years since we had that insurance, so I had to update everything. I looked up and watched Anna roll around a corner and out of sight.

I know I got my gurney-charging-down-the-hall imagery from cliché TV scenes, but, as for the orderly, he was me. Or, I should say, he came from me acting on a soap opera called *As the World Turns*. I played him on about twenty episodes in the first few years I was living in New York City, pursuing an acting career. I never had more than two or three lines in any one episode; usually lines like "I'll get the towels," or "Come this way, Mr. Munson," or "Your daughter's in good hands now." I didn't have a character name other than "Orderly," but it was a nice day's pay at the time, and I would get to be in the closing credits. In one episode, Orderly found himself written into a pivotal moment: bribed by a scandalous patient, he helps her sneak out of the hospital by helicopter under the cover of night. That week, I even got named in *Soap Opera Digest* in an "Upcoming Episodes" column. At twenty-four, nothing could have been cooler.

We wrapped up the insurance paperwork, and I moved in the direction I saw Anna go. As I took a few steps up a hallway, I heard the Velcro rip of a blood pressure cuff. I followed it and found the room where Anna was. A doctor and nurse were flanking her. My father stood against the wall. Anna was already on a bed, cleats on the floor, laces still tied. She seemed to be hyperventilating. The nurse was rubbing her inner arm with alcohol, preparing to take blood. The doctor looked twenty. I remembered then what my aunt told me to say.

"She's demonstrating a mix of cardiac and respiratory," I recited. "Possible extrapyramidal effects. Or signs of cardiac arrythmia."

The doctor looked at me, then said he agreed.

"Are you a doctor?" he asked me.

"No."

"What do you do?"

I used to hate that question, no matter where I was, even in moments like this. For so long, the truth was always too long (and embarrassing) to tell: "I'm an aspiring playwright, screenwriter, and actor. Also, to survive, I'm an adjunct lecturer, office assistant, receptionist, typist in a periodontists' office, and high school baseball coach...someone who would like to make an actual living at what he wants to do, but can't quite do it, so I have seven jobs."

However, this was the first year in my life I had a full-time faculty position, so my answer could be simple. I told him.

"Where?" the doctor asked.

"Mercy College in Dobbs Ferry."

Anna sat bolt upright and looked at me.

"Here it comes," she said. Her eyes were wide, and she began to rock. "Daddy, it's happening again. Alligators."

"Alligators?" I said. "What does that mean?"

Her face turned red. She grabbed the nurse's arms and seemed to struggle to breathe. The nurse held her through it. My father said he'd wait for Kristen in the lobby. I knew he was leaving because he thought something unwatchable might be about to happen here.

The doctor followed him, then returned with another doctor a moment later. This was an older man, silver haired, bespectacled, clearly in charge.

"Well, hi there," he said to Anna, who had eased back down. She said a breathy hello back. "You just relax, okay?"

"Okay," she said.

"What did you say about alligators, Anna?" I asked again.

"They were coming," Anna answered.

The doctor turned toward me.

"We've put in for an immediate chest x-ray and EKG."

Heart attack, I thought to myself.

Then, he asked me for Anna's history.

By now, we had a well-honed script of Anna's medical history. I told the doctor about her seizure cluster at five months, the different theories we'd been told as to the cause, and all the meds, diets, and vitamins she'd been on since. He asked the drug names. I rattled them off, noting the one or two that brought bad reactions. It was always a lot for anyone to keep up with, even an experienced emergency room doctor, but I kept going.

Anna was quickly back from the x-ray.

"Anna?" the older doctor said tenderly. "Tell me about the alligators."

I told him she also said something about seeing sharks at the field.

"They come at me," she said.

"And then, your breathing is difficult?" he asked.

"Yes."

The doctor was quiet a moment, just watching her, thinking. I watched him watch her, as if I'd see into his mind as it sifted through the lessons of a career in emergency medicine, alighting on the answer I wanted to hear: "Ah, yes. I see. Nope! These are not seizures. Don't sweat it. Nothing's changed. We see this sometimes. She needs to stop eating such and such, or drinking such and such.... Should be all gone tomorrow, and you can happily go back to the wrenching nights you're used to. In fact, if you move it, you can even make it back to the game right now for the last inning. Maybe she can get an at-bat!"

"It's scary when this happens, huh?" he continued with Anna.

"Yes."

"Was today the first time you noticed these things? Alligators? Or sharks?"

"No."

I looked at her now. What?

"When did you see these things before?" the doctor said.

"Like, last week," she said, wearily. "I told you, Dad."

I said she most definitely did not tell me that sharks or alligators were coming at her. Most definitely not. The doctor put his hand on my arm, as if he thought I was getting upset.

"In science class, remember?" Anna added. "I told you on the way home that something scary happened."

Anna and I talked a lot, especially in the car. Thanks to my class times, I was able to drive her and two kids who live nearby to school every morning. We called ourselves "The Breakfast Club."

Depending on my schedule, sometimes, I could take them home in the afternoons too. It could be a lot of back and forth from my classes in Westchester or Harlem back to Queens, and it put a lot of miles on my leased Corolla, but it was a way to keep an ear to the ground with what was going on with the kids, both gossip wise and academically.

I worried whether Anna would be able to continue to make friends and get through the middle school transition socially without losing too many feathers. I myself had nothing but unpleasant memories of middle school, and I was afraid for her. Whether it was damage from seizures, side effects of whatever drug she was on, or the disrupted area of her brain, Anna sometimes had trouble putting words in the order she intended. It hadn't been a problem for her socially before, but I worried about how this would come across in middle school. So far, so good.

I must have missed this report about whatever happened in science that day. Maybe I was on my phone or answering student emails as she got into the car. Maybe I was grading papers. Maybe music was playing too loud. Maybe I tuned her out, figured it was something unimportant. Scary stuff can always happen in science class, like Bunsen burner fires, eviscerated frogs, pop quizzes...but still, I felt like sharks and alligators would have gotten my attention.

"I don't remember that, Anna. I think I would have remembered if you told me that."

"It wasn't sharks that time," Anna said. "I told you I fell off a car."

"You fell off a car?" the doctor stepped closer to her. "What do you mean?"

"I saw a car coming at me, then I was on top of it, and I fell."

My father came back in with Kristen. She moved quickly to Anna and hugged her.

"I love you," Kristen said, kissing Anna's head.

"I love you too," Anna replied. "Will I be better for tonight?"

Kristen looked at me, then down at the floor.

"Well, we have to make sure we know what's going on so we can fix it," she said, stroking Anna's hair.

"What's tonight?" I asked.

"Competition!" Anna said, smiling like she felt bad for the idiot who could forget such a thing.

"Tonight?"

"Yes!" she said.

I had forgotten, but now I understood what Anna had meant about the floppy ballet hands. Her studio company was competing at an event on Long Island.

"I don't think that's on the agenda tonight for us, Anna," I said.

Anna turned to Kristen.

"I'm missing it?"

She was instantly in tears. I realized she hadn't cried once all morning. If I were her, I'd have cried a lot by now. I remember crying all the time as a kid. I never had more than a few colds and flus in my childhood, and no doubt, I cried through all of them. I had the Chickenpox, and I remember I cried as much as I itched.

I was sensitive, but I could never remember crying over missing a baseball game. Whether it was injury, sickness, rainout, or some rare family occasion my parents deemed unmissable, I never minded. There'd always be another game. Just as there'd be more dance competitions, which I said then to Anna, but she still looked heartbroken.

"I've never missed competition," she said, miserably.

The doctor asked us to step outside the small room into the hall. A nurse stayed with Anna.

"I want to preface this by saying I'm not Neurology," he said. "But I'm not convinced what we are seeing are seizures. I understand she has her seizures at night?"

"Yes," I said. I was so relieved to hear this that I felt like I was floating. "For about seven years now. All during sleep."

"What I'm seeing seems to have another element."

He said we should transfer her to Cohen Children's Hospital up the road.

"What other element?" I asked. "Side effects?"

"I don't think so. Side effects usually happen in the introduction period of a medication. She's been on everything she's currently taking for a while. The chest x-ray, the EKG all read normal."

"There's no heart attack. That's clear?" I said.

"Yes," he said. "But panic attacks can look like seizures and, in fact, look and feel like heart attacks," the doctor went on. "The hallucinations do concern me, but I'm going to guess there's an anxiety element here. I think what we're seeing is panic attacks."

He said they would order an ambulance for the transfer.

Panic attacks. Not seizures now coming in the daytime. I was almost giddy. The terrible change in her epilepsy may not have come at all. Anxiety? Who would blame any of us for having anxiety? Makes sense to me. Surely, that's it. And surely, we could deal with that!

CHAPTER TWO

WELCOME AND UNWELCOME THINGS

W hen I was a kid, they called middle school "junior high school," and not only did I see my first seizure there, I also had my first crush. I was a low-performing student, even in Home Economics, and most of my interest was to play the dopey, funny jock. In an effort to prevent my bad habits and lowly self-image from becoming permanent, my parents would try all-boys Catholic school as a kind of reformatory. I took an entry test and squeaked off the waitlist into the very strict and demanding Chaminade High School in Nassau County. It did end up keeping me out of major behavioral trouble, and I went to college, much thanks to baseball, but I never really stopped wondering about the quiet, long-haired girl who always smiled at me back in junior high, even after I blew my chance with her.

For some reason I may never understand, Kristen Barthel, at thirteen, found me just as likeable as I found her, and we knew this by way of that ancient theatrical convention: the messenger. I had a friend from the eighth-grade baseball team willing to courier verbal messages between us until it came time to move things to a more serious level: the phone call. I delayed for weeks, but finally, one afternoon from my parents' bedroom rotary phone, I called the number my messenger had scored for me, and which I'd memorized like a song. Despite being ready with an index card listing preplanned conversation starters, upon hearing Kristen's voice, I lost all nerve. I may have mumbled off a few of my prepared bullet points: "What's your favorite TV show?" or "What do you like to do on weekends?" but I got off that phone as fast as possible. She called me back a few days later, I suppose to give me a second chance, but faced with the risk of flopping again, I bailed. I refused to accept the call, even telling my mother, who was standing there holding the receiver toward me, that I had no idea who this "Kristen" was.

Then, over the next four years, Kristen blossomed into one of the most beautiful and popular students in her high school. She had high grades and a handsome wrestling team captain boyfriend headed to Brown. I was a C+ class clown and, like most of my classmates, when it came to female companionship, had to rely on imagination and romantic fantasy for the future. Eventually, of course, I dated people, but through the years, after every miserable breakup, and there were plenty, I found myself thinking back to Kristen and my great romantic blunder in junior high.

A few years into my floundering acting life in the city, I took a crack at screenwriting. I'd learned a bit about moviemaking by then. I'd been lucky enough to play the lead in a small independent film called *Too Much Sleep*. It would end up doing that rare thing for indie projects: making it. It got great reviews, ended up in theatres all over the country, then on cable TV, and fetched some major award nominations. It didn't make me famous, but it did expose me to screenwriting, and soon after, I wrote my first script.

I used me and Kristen as its basis. My script told the story of a depressed former pitcher who hangs out with a famous literary character, Samuel Coleridge's Ancient Mariner, at a Long Island pizzeria. He gets to apologize to a girl named Kristen for missing his long-ago chance with her, hoping, maybe, for another shot. By an absurd series of lucky strokes, the movie was made in Los Angeles and starred a handful of famous names like Jennifer Love Hewitt, Dash Mihok, and Peter Facinelli. Miramax Films released *Telling You* a few years later. *Variety* called it "a good start" for the creative team. I wasn't thrilled with the changes made to the script before shooting, and had nothing to do with the actual making of the movie beyond selling the screenplay for a few thousand bucks, but that's show business, I learned. I did option a couple scripts to production companies in Hollywood in the years following, but from that point, I invested myself mostly in writing stage plays. In the theatre, only the playwright has the right to change the script. Still, I was glad *Variety* didn't hate it and felt lucky as hell to have a movie produced. Plus, it was nice to make a bit of money as a writer at twenty-five.

When *Telling You* came out, I lived in Manhattan with two of my closest theatre friends, Michael Laurence and George Demas, in a Hell's Kitchen railroad apartment. I survived check-to-check on the "survival jobs" I worked, like an office assistant job at my father's small insurance agency. Despite having been the lead actor in a critically-acclaimed movie, becoming a bona fide Hollywood screenwriter, having a play I wrote produced at the Beckett Theatre on Theatre Row, doing soap operas, a few commercials, and becoming a member of the actors' unions, I still relied on a job that involved answering phones, making deli runs for salesmen, and clearing jams in the copier. I was lonely, too, fresh out of yet another breakup.

Then, one day, as I sat at the office receptionist desk, it hit me.

Maybe Kristen of Long Island's West Hollow Junior High School Class of 1985 was still out there, willing to receive one more message from me. Maybe if she got a letter in the mail that let her know a real movie based on our eighth-grade romantic near-miss was sitting in every Blockbuster Video store in America that week, she might be up for a coffee with me.

Of course, it was a vainglorious endeavor with all kinds of red flags, but with the passionate support of my roommates, I went ahead with it. Though I had only dialed it once all those years ago, I still had her phone number memorized. With that and a quick Google search, I found what appeared to be Kristen's parents' address. Michael and George were as starved for excitement as I was, so all three of us went to the mailbox to drop my letter, then pooled our pocket money, went somewhere cheap, and toasted the unknown future. About a month later, Kristen and I met at a café near Union Square. She, too, was newly single, and every bit the person I remembered. Michael and George would both be in our wedding party a year and a half later.

Anna was born the summer of our fifth year of marriage. I had recently gotten the teaching offer at CCNY and by then had published a couple plays. My newest one was days from premiering at the Axis Theatre in the West Village when Kristen went into labor. There was a dress rehearsal that very night, and I was holding the script I'd still be making edits on as I watched my first child come into the world at Lenox Hill Hospital, a full-term, uneventful birth. She had a thatch of bright blonde hair, like mine.

*

The ambulance took a while to arrive for the transfer to Cohen's. It would have been faster for us just to drive Anna in our own car, but that's not how they do official transfers. It was two hours before they made all the arrangements and loaded Anna up and on her way. Since their cars were in the hospital lot, Kristen and my father would meet us there. I rode along with Anna and the EMTs.

I held as tight as I could to the ER doctor's suggestion that this was something other than seizures. If this were all a matter of Anna worrying, or some early pubescent surge of emotions, it meant that her seizures were still nocturnal and hadn't begun attacking her waking life. Part of me hadn't even completely given up on her missing tonight's dance competition.

Few people in my life would call me an optimist, but when I needed to find a ray of promise to stave off despair about Anna, I could hunt pretty darn hard for one. For most of the year, her seizures had been coming every single night, which is why we had been increasing the med dosage, but as I had reported to her neurologist, the seizures themselves actually seemed to be shorter. Rather than the ninety-second, violent sneak attack they'd been for so long, lately, they were less abrupt, with a less kinetic peak. She'd sit up slowly in bed, stare ahead for a few seconds, then begin to bob, like she was moving to the beat of a pleasant children's melody. She'd have a few quick, upper body twitches, like chills, then relax and drift back to sleep. From what I knew of the different sorts of seizures, these seemed to me to be "myoclonic" rather than her usual "complex partial," since the body rigidity, the clenched extremities, the kicking, and flailing wouldn't come. I had been determined to take this change as encouraging. This was what her final childhood seizures must look like in their diminishment, I thought to myself. The beginning of a happy end.

There was some logic behind this thinking. At five months old, NewYork-Presbyterian had originally diagnosed the cause as a brain lesion, a condition called "cortical dysplasia." A hard-to-see area of brain tissue in her frontal lobe evidently had not formed properly in utero. It wasn't genetic; just a random accident like a birthmark on a forearm. Cortical dysplasia, we were informed, was a common cause of epilepsy. The relative good news was, it wasn't progressive, like a tumor. The bad news was, short of invasive surgery, it would always be there.

But then, a change came. When Anna was two, we switched her treatment to another hospital. There, at NYU, a new MRI was taken. It was the first since she was five months old. It suggested, to all our surprise, a very good thing. The problem area, first identified as a lesion, seemed to have shrunk. If it was a lesion, it shouldn't have changed size at all. Our new doctor and the neuroimaging expert who looked at the films agreed the condition was not as originally thought. Anna did not have cortical dysplasia, they inferred, but rather a disorder called "delayed myelination." This was also a common cause of epilepsy, especially in childhood. Essentially, it meant that some of Anna's brain tissue wasn't fully insulated yet, as it should have been at birth, so it was leaking electrical impulses. If this delayed myelination was causing the seizures, and the affected area was shrinking, it could mean that things were still in progress, still completing. After two years of thinking Anna's condition was permanent, we could hope that this would all fade away in late childhood or adolescence.

Now at Cohen's, we were given a private room on the Pediatric Neurology floor. I knew from experience that if I didn't make it clear that we were *not requesting* a private room, I'd receive a big bill for it in a few months, since our insurance plan doesn't cover "luxury" extras. I was told it's the only room available that was equipped with the overnight video equipment, so I shouldn't worry, there would be no extra fee. I knew I'd get the big bill anyway. One way or another, we were fortunate. Hospital stays were bad enough, but they were at their worst when only a lightweight curtain divided one anguished family from another in a space the size of a typical bedroom, especially with Anna's nighttime seizures. This room not only had the usual: the mounted television, the adjustable bed, the overnight futon chair for a parent to sleep on, but also its own bathroom with a shower.

The nurse whose shift would last through the night introduced herself and took Anna's vitals. Technicians hooked up the EEG monitors and began to glue the electrode leads to her head, chest, and back. Anna had always loathed this process, but she bit her lip and let the television distract. The nurse reviewed Anna's medicine regimen and said the floor pediatrician would be in to see us soon. My father asked if we'd like him to go on a food run to a nearby diner, and Anna jumped at his offer.

"Yes! Cheeseburger and fries!"

I looked at Kristen, who was already looking at me. I knew what this meant, and I felt a pang of anger. Kristen was currently committed to the idea that a strict gluten-free diet would reduce seizures, and this would be a flagrant violation.

We had tried countless treatments on Anna, and nothing ever stopped the seizures or even alleviated them for long. And anyway, it was hard to tell what might be having an effect. There were always multiple factors at work, so any real scientific observation of the effect of any single med, combination of meds, diet, etc. was impossible. For instance, if Anna had a night with no seizures, our response was to make sure we did everything we'd done that day exactly the same the next day. Maybe it had been a change in med dosage, maybe it was that she didn't watch television that evening, maybe it was even the gluten-free diet finally kicking in, some vitamin, the meds given at nine rather than eight, etc. But then, the next night, she could have any number of seizures, when we had done everything the same.

There were always so many fads, rumors, and new studies coming at us from so many directions. It was often a challenge for Kristen and me to come to agreement on what to try and what to ignore or when to give up on something. Add exhaustion to the mix, and there could be serious tension. I had no doubt that we still shared the hope that one of these solutions would prove the miracle discovery, but the years of letdowns, the fear of hoping for anything too much, and having each other right there to take it all out on, Kristen and I could feel like two people using each other as proverbial punching bags.

I knew damn well I was being unfair, but before Kristen could say a word about the food, I announced that Anna would be having a big fat cheeseburger, and all the "damned carb-filled fries she wants," and that our gluten-free diet experiment had obviously come to its end. Kristen's eyebrows rose, high. We'd argue later, no doubt, and it would feel perfectly normal to do so. Over the years, we learned many statistics about epilepsy. One was that parents of epilepsy patients have divorce rates far higher than the norm.

"Yes!" Anna cheered when I approved the burger. She threw her arms up in celebration and a finger caught a wire, ripping some leads off, which then got stuck in her hair. She laughed, as did the technician. Then, we all laughed. I felt like we were already making progress on stress reduction. Here we were, laughing in intensive care, and Anna had been liberated from the gluten-free diet she hated. It put limitations on her every day, and nothing killed a friend's birthday party like having to bring her own specially-packed (tasteless, according to her) meal and slice of quasi-cake. Even that morning in the car, she had protested bitterly as I extracted the egg from her Kaiser roll.

"Well now it's not an egg *sandwich* Dad, is it?"

"No. But it's egg, Anna."

"That's right! It's egg. Just a flat sheet of egg."

"With cheese," I added.

"Most of that melted into the roll. It's mostly egg."

"Well, try to enjoy your nice flat sheet of mostly egg, Anna. And thank Grandpa for bringing it too."

"And you enjoy your nice, round egg and cheese *sandwich*, Dad," she said. I didn't look, but I was sure the eyes rolled and the mouth twisted into a tweenager sneer. "And thank you, Grandpa. You tried."

Kristen had silently relented on the gluten. I nodded and smiled, thanking her. She nodded back, slightly. My father took food orders and headed out. Anna held the television remote, which was connected by a rubber wire to the wall behind her. By now, she knew hospital television systems well. She started to channel surf, stopping on a Disney movie she'd already seen twenty times called *The Princess and The Frog*. She looked content lying there, despite the stench of the EEG technician's glue. She hadn't had an episode of whatever this was since we got into the ambulance. If we were home, this could have been a Saturday Anna might have chosen over softball: lying down, propped up by puffy pillows on a bed, remote in hand, diner food on the way.

I checked my phone and saw an email from the neurologist at NYU. It said she'd already left a message with the head of Neurology here at Cohen's. I wrote back that according to the ER doctor, Anna wasn't having seizures but panic attacks but that they're doing a video EEG anyway. A woman who looked young enough to be one of my freshman students entered the room. She introduced herself as the resident pediatrician on the floor.

"Hello, Anna," she said. "How are you?"

"Good," Anna said, casually, eyes on the movie.

"Well, she hasn't had her best day," I said. "But she's comfy now, right Anna?"

"Yep."

"Feeling better?" the doctor asked her.

"Yep."

"That's good to hear," the doctor continued. "Mom, Dad, the neurologist on call will be here to see Anna in a little while. Until then, we'll get everything set up for the overnight."

"I'm staying overnight?" Anna said, turning her eyes toward us, her facial expression now wretched.

"Yes, Anna," I said, apologetically.

"But I have dance."

"We just need to take a nice look at things," the doctor answered. "Hopefully, we can get what we need and release you sometime Monday."

Monday. Ouch, I thought to myself. That's two nights.

The doctor told Anna she was delighted to meet her, then asked us to step into the hall to give her history.

"Mom?" Anna called out as we followed the doctor. Her wires stretched as she turned her head toward us and the technician backed off again.

"Yes, sweetheart?"

"Tell them I can't miss dance tonight."

"I know, honey," Kristen said softly. "But I think we have to."

Anna closed her eyes. I tried not to look at her. The EEG technician asked her to try to keep her head still. We turned back again and headed into the hall. We had only taken a few steps when we heard Anna calling for help. We all three turned heel and rushed back into the room.

She was in it again—pale, panting, looking terrified.

"Anna?" the doctor said. "Tell me what you're feeling."

She placed her stethoscope on Anna's chest.

"It's coming again," Anna said.

"What's coming?"

Anna screamed and twisted back toward the wall behind her, as if trying to take cover. She shielded her eyes with one hand and with the other pointed back at the television. We looked up. The same movie. She'd seen it twenty times at home. Maybe more.

On the screen, dancing with cartoon frogs in a New Orleans lagoon, was Louis, the horn-playing cartoon alligator.

*

By the time my father returned from the diner, we'd spoken extensively to both the resident and the pediatric neurologist on call. The resident seemed to feel that what Anna was displaying, even with the hallucinations (what she called the "psychotic features"), all aligned with what the ER doctor had said: this was an "anxiety situation." She told us that she sees a good deal of these cases, particularly in girls Anna's age, when puberty begins. She reiterated that panic attacks could look like seizures, even trigger them. I still felt that this was the best diagnosis we could hope for today, so I was encouraged to hear this was her hunch too.

SHE DANCED WITH LIGHTNING

But after the pediatrician moved on to another patient, the neurologist arrived and burst my bubble. He gave Anna a basic neurological exam, asking her to touch her nose, resist his pressure on her arms, move her eyes left and right, etc., then listened to the history I'd now given a third time that day. I told him what I had seen in the car, repeated my aunt's vocabulary, then what Anna had said about sharks and how she just reacted to the alligator in the movie.

"Sounds like seizures to me," he said.

It was a gut punch.

"Not panic attacks?" I said. "We've been hearing that all day."

"In Anna's case, I would assume not, considering her condition," he said. "But we'll see on the EEG. That's why we're here."

What he was saying contradicted both doctors we'd seen that day but, if correct, would be the worst news we'd had in nine years.

The doctor explained that for the next two days, our job would be to watch Anna and press the red "event button" on the end of a long rubber cord whenever anything happened. This would mark the time on the EEG readout and video, which was being taken from an overhead night vision camera. We agreed that Kristen would go home and bring Nora to the dance competition. I was told there was no attending neurologist on Sundays, so it would be Monday morning before we'd know what they saw inside Anna's brain.

My mother arrived. She had Nora, whom she'd picked up from dance class, still in her leotard. Nora, the usually garrulous, humorous little kid, was quiet. Seeing her sister wired up to a hospital bed was nothing new to her, but I knew it affected her intensely. Anna said hello, and Nora leaned over the side of the bed and hugged her legs.

"I have to miss competition tonight," Anna said. Nora said nothing in return, but crawled onto the bed beside her.

"My stomach hurts," Nora said.

"You're probably hungry," I said to her.

"I ate a big breakfast."

Nora had stomach pains often. They'd always pass after some rest, but they happened frequently enough that we had her checked by a few specialists over the years. None of them found anything wrong.

Since my father had returned with the food, the room was feeling crowded. I had no appetite, and took the opportunity of Anna being well attended to go down to the lobby. I needed time to sort out how this turn of events would rearrange my next few days' work plans. Monday was my day off at Mercy, but I still taught a screenwriting class at City College and would need to find someone to step in for me. First, however, I'd have to cancel my private baseball lessons for Sunday. This was another job I had. I coached a travel team of fifteen-year-old boys in summertime, but also worked all year round as a private one-on-one pitching coach. Tonight, Coach Marc would have to text four very devoted little league parents and reschedule. Tomorrow, Professor Marc would deal with the problem of his Monday screenwriting class.

The hospital's main lobby was big, quiet, and lit up by the still-sunny day through a glass ceiling. There was an area of padded seats that circled a babbling fountain basin, and for the first time since the ambulance, I sat down. I was anxious enough as it was, but now, facing these next days and nights hunkered down in a hospital, I felt a bit overwhelmed. The more I thought about the week ahead, the worse it got, and my own stomach hurt. There were tomorrow's baseball lessons and the cash I'd lose out on. The class at City College only met once a week, so canceling it wasn't an option; it would put the students too far behind so close to the end of the term. Kristen's students had their standardized state exams coming up, so there was no way she could take Monday off to be here, and I couldn't even bring myself to consider the possibility of having to stay over into Tuesday, when I had even more classes at Mercy plus rehearsal with the theatre club, of which I was faculty advisor. Then I thought of Anna missing two days of her own schoolwork, and I felt like screaming.

I wasn't sure exactly how to word my texts just yet. I anticipated a lengthy back and forth with each parent if I was to mention anything alarming about my daughter, and I didn't want to have to give explanations. So, I put it off. Instead, despite my Aunt Maureen once telling me to never do it, I Googled. I typed in *seizures, adolescence, myoclonic, hallucinations,* and before long, I was convinced that Anna had some degenerative syndrome, like Lennox Gastaut, Unverricht-Lundborg, Juvenile Neuronal Ceroid Lipofuscinosis, or Huntington's Disease. One stood out above the rest. I read for half an hour about Lafora Disease, a rare and terminal genetic epilepsy, whose onset matched every symptom we'd seen that day. If Anna had Lafora, I read, we could expect a "relentless cognitive decline," with life expectancy at another ten to fifteen years. One article extract I read on Lafora even said "extrapyramidal" somewhere in it.

In these cases, some gene lying in wait until about Anna's age would trigger the brain to basically fall apart. Natural processes, until then showing no signs of trouble, slam into reverse. Instead of development and growth, there is decline and decay. I recalled something I learned about biology at one of my many past day jobs, the one as a typist for the periodontists. The doctors would dictate detailed letters into a tape recorder, and my job was to put them to paper. They were case letters to the patient's referring dentist, to keep them informed as to the procedures performed. It was nature, pure nature, and it was disgusting. The mouth, I learned, is a hopeless battleground, the only possibility being to valiantly delay the inevitable, our age of "sans teeth," as Shakespeare put it. Gums recede, roots loosen and disintegrate, teeth rot and break—and people bleed, ooze, and ache until the end. These neurological syndromes I was reading about on the internet cause the brain to do just that—melt, essentially, into total failure.

I got off the internet. Everyone knows that Googling symptoms is a masochistic thing to do, especially during a mysterious medical crisis with your epileptic pre-adolescent child.

I thought back to my baseball parents and started typing the first text.

I'M SORRY I NEED TO CANCEL TOMORROW MORNING'S LESSON. MY DAUGHTER IS SICK

Even that was too much information. I deleted it.

I'M SORRY I NEED TO CANCEL TOMORROW MORNING'S...

Looking at the small letters on the phone made the back of my eyes hurt. Now I was nauseous. I slowly finished what I started.

...LESION

Well look at that, I thought. Tomorrow morning's lesion. How charming. "Autocorrect" has a dark sense of humor. After a few times retyping, it let me fix it.

...LESSON

I took a deep breath and set my eyes on the water splashing in the fountain for a moment. It's really a nice little pool, I thought, then typed on.

NOT ONLY TOMORROW'S LESSON BUT ALL LESSONS EVER. MY DAUGHTER HAS SOMETHING TERRIBLE LIKE LAFORA DISEASE. I ALWAYS KNEW IT WOULD COME TO SOMETHING LIKE THIS. I KNEW IT.

Despite the nausea, it felt good to write that for some reason. Then I felt ashamed. What am I doing? I thought to myself. We'd had every kind of blood and DNA test available over the years. They would have seen these syndromes if they were there. These must be panic attacks, they must be. All will be good.

I'M SORRY BUT I NEED TO CANCEL TOMORROW MORNING'S LESSON. SOMETHING HAS COME UP WITH MY DAUGHTER. NOTHING SERIOUS. ALL IS GOOD. I'LL BE IN TOUCH THIS WEEK. ALL IS GOOD.

I sent it, then copied, pasted, and sent to the next parent. Then the next. I then realized I'd written "all is good" twice.

I was so nauseous by now, I felt I might vomit. I put the phone in my pocket, swung my legs up and lay down across four seats.

"She gets up to play softball, and now she's in the hospital for days," I said to myself. "The poor kid. She's turning twelve. Her stupid father has to sleep on her floor."

I was sweating. Breathing fast. I closed my eyes.

"But they said they're not seizures! Two doctors said so! She's stressed out! That's it! We'll fix it all!" I was speaking aloud. I knew people were looking, but I didn't stop. "So maybe it *is* all good, and we'll figure it out. Yes. All is good. It's a new life from here on. All is good. All is good. All is good."

I heard the text pings from my pocket and took out the phone. I knew it was the little league parents wanting to reschedule, or wishing me good luck with my daughter. I wanted to turn off the ringer, but I didn't. I needed to hear it if Kristen called from the room and told me to come running. For me, ever since Anna started having seizures, the cell phone in my pocket was like a live grenade. The call could come anytime, the ring or vibration, and with it, all hell.

*

There's a quote I always loved from Shakespeare's *Macbeth*. The character Macduff says it late in the play. To me, it pretty much sums up human life:

> *Such welcome and unwelcome things at once*
> *'Tis hard to reconcile.*

I'm guessing that for most parents, their eleven-year-old having an acute anxiety disorder would land squarely in the very much "unwelcome" category of things. For me, considering what I first thought was now happening to her, it was most welcome. Early Monday afternoon, another neurologist came into the hospital room with her report. She said she'd reviewed the EEG and video of the prior two nights, closely checking all thirty or so spots where I pressed the red button and that while Anna's usual nocturnal seizures were there, none of the other episodes showed epileptic spikes. These were panic attacks indeed, she said.

"It's a serious thing," she explained. "But we don't think they are seizures."

I hadn't slept since Saturday. I stayed up both nights beside Anna's hospital bed battling the temptation to read more about Lafora and the other hideous diseases I'd found. Instead, I stared out the window at pouring rain. I also read, sometimes two or three times over, the student play manuscripts that would be workshopped in my class and sent critiques to the generous adjunct covering for me today. After that, I just stared at Anna sleeping, waiting for "events." A few looked like the shorter nocturnal seizures I'd been seeing lately, and some looked like she was having nightmares. I pushed the button for all of them.

Kristen arrived just in time for the conversation with the neurologist. She had taken a half day at her school.

"Are we sure everything yesterday was not seizure activity?" Kristen asked.

Kristen always asked many questions, and I knew more would be coming. I worried one would eventually be met with an answer to spoil the good I was hearing in this news. I just wanted to nod and go home.

"That's what they're saying, Kristen," I said.

"Well we can't be sure that a panic attack didn't lead to a seizure," the doctor said. "You'll follow up with your regular neurologist. I spoke with her this morning, and we agreed to discharge Anna now, get you guys home. She wants to start Anna on a different medication."

"I feel like we've tried just about every one there is," I said. "Is there any point in trying another?"

"That would be for you to discuss with your regular neurologist. She wants you to call the office to make an appointment."

Kristen asked another.

"The hallucinations were part of the panic attack?"

A woman had been standing behind the neurologist. I hadn't yet looked closely at her ID badge, assuming she was another resident or a medical student shadowing the rounds. She stepped forward.

"Very likely," she said. "Hallucinations, voices, fear, scary thoughts...all of this is common."

She explained she was a social worker and handed us pamphlets and one-sheets about anxiety in adolescents.

"Has she been pretty stressed out? About school? That's often a major stressor."

"Not particularly. In fact," I said, then finding myself feeling humorous. "Sometimes we wish she'd stress out a little *more* about school."

Anna has said many times that she couldn't care less what her grades were like, as long as she "passes." Bayside is a high-ranking NYC school district, with a number of the top high schools in the city. We knew plenty of parents who would be mortified if their child had Anna's attitude, and scoff at our failure to influence it, but we felt there wasn't much more we could do than what we were already doing. Work was hard for Anna. Studying for a quiz or test took much repetition. From the start, we insisted she be placed in an "ICT" class (Integrated Co-Teaching) where there's a special education teacher assisting a lead teacher so that she got extra assistance and time to ensure her performance met grade level. Homework was enormously time-consuming, and energy-consuming, and with her extracurricular activities like dance, always accomplished in a rush. Because of all she had to deal with from the cognitive effects of her medications, we were satisfied that she was doing as well as she was. Of the three marking periods of her first middle school year, she'd made honor roll for two of them.

Nora did just about all her own work on her own, but Kristen and I had to review Anna's assignment agenda every day, help her keep track of due dates, and study with her. She protested through all of it. But wasn't that a normal thing with kids? Don't many do anything, say anything, to avoid work? I now wondered if we were to blame. Had we been asking too much of her to get her work done adequately? I sure knew it was stressful for Kristen and me, but I was now wondering if we had pushed Anna too hard.

"She's turning twelve too," the social worker went on. "Hormones. Middle school. And if something is inherent, this is about the age many people start to exhibit psychic symptoms, whatever may have triggered it."

Psychic symptoms. A chilling ring to that. Still, I thought to myself, these weren't daytime seizures. No matter what the social worker might say about all this, I still wasn't ready to surrender my sense of relief in that.

"And of course, she's lived with epilepsy all her life. I'm sure that's tremendously stressful, to her and you."

You. Us. Kristen. Nora. Me. Of course, all I've known is a state of emergency since before the kid could crawl. Every night is a high-stakes adventure. Who could possibly have survived in our house *without* a stress disorder? Our plants were probably stressed. Come to think of it, they never really lasted long. Nora got unexplained stomach pains. All kinds of household mysteries were being solved here.

"What about school?" I asked. "Should we keep her home tomorrow?"

"No," the social worker said. "We want things to stay as normal as possible."

"But if this happens at school..."

"It's overwhelmingly likely that it won't," she said. "Typically, they'll have panic attacks in safe environments. Near you, or a family member. When they know the support is there."

She told us this is all treatable. Usually most effectively with psychotherapy.

"She'll have to learn techniques to calm herself, to recognize symptoms and be in close touch with her body. Methodical deep breathing is an example, which works very well."

An hour or so later, Anna's leads were removed. She was able to shower while Kristen and I packed to leave.

"We'll all learn about it," I said. "We'll change our whole life. Get a new perspective. Slow it all down."

"I want another opinion." Kristen said, stonily.

"Of course. But starting today, we gotta bring it all down a notch. Everything," I said. I wasn't sure I was making any sense. "All the worry, the tension between us.... I think we've seen the damage done to this kid, and we gotta stop it now."

By the time all was in order for discharge, it was afternoon. We carried our things into the hall. Anna was walking slowly a few paces ahead of us.

"Anna, how do you feel?" Kristen asked.

"Not good," she said.

"Why not?"

"Because."

"Anna," I said. "You weren't having seizures. This is good news! Do you understand how good that news is?"

"No."

"Well it is. We will figure out how to calm down and be okay, alright?"

"Not okay for me," she said.

"Yes for you! Why do you say that?"

"Because if they weren't seizures, I could have gone to competition," she said. She had a silver medal in her hand. The company number placed second, and they sent Nora home with a medal for her. "I missed it for no reason."

"Well, it wasn't exactly *no reason* Anna," I replied. "And there will be lots of competitions."

"You keep saying that," she said.

"Sure I do," I said. "Because it's true. Next time, there's no way you'll miss."

"*Next* time," Anna snarled.

Down the hall, an elevator opened. Four or five members of Anna's softball team came pouring out. When they saw Anna, they turned and ran toward her, calling her name. Anna tottered back and grabbed Kristen's arm, hard.

"What's the matter, honey? Your friends are here! I guess they came right after school together!"

Anna didn't answer but began to shake.

"They're scaring me," Anna said.

"Scaring you, how?"

"Mommy. My heart..."

The kids were almost to her, with smiles and arms thrown open.

"Breathe, sweetheart," Kristen said. Anna inhaled and forced a smile. Her face turned red.

"It's okay, sweetheart," I said. "It's not a seizure. It's nothing. Just breathe. Breathe."

CHAPTER THREE

CAMPUS

W e called and made our follow-up appointment with Anna's neurologist for the soonest available time slot at NYU, which was in ten days. Until then, she wanted us to maintain the Lacosamide dose as it was and to start adding another medicine called Clobazam. She would email the prescription. Regardless of whether these were panic attacks, she felt we had given Lacosamide the old college try, and it was time for another. This would be medication number eight in Anna's career. The process for introducing it would be the usual: once the new Clobazam reached a "therapeutic level" in the blood, we'd start withdrawing the current Lacosamide. Until then, she'd be taking both, plus the marijuana pills.

In the meantime, we planned to move fast to find a psychotherapist and change our home into a low-stress, healing serenity center. I regretted that the softball game and dance competition were casualties, but I felt a refreshed enthusiasm. For some reason, I was confident we could handle this, maybe because I felt responsible for causing it. It was evident that Anna had been damaged by living with parents who were failing to mask their own worries, heartache, and helplessness, and I was looking at this diagnosis as a wake-up call.

Anna didn't seize overnight into Tuesday. She and Nora were dressing for school as I made the usual eggs and mango chunk breakfast. Kristen was headed out the door for work.

"We need an appointment for the second opinion," she said, like this was firmly decided. "Julie got a recommendation of someone at NewYork-Presbyterian."

Julie's daughters were dancers who attended the same studio. She was a lawyer and had given Kristen the name of a pediatric neurologist she'd been referred to by a top neurosurgeon named Theodore Schwartz, whom she'd consulted for expert testimony in medical cases. I didn't see a need for this, since we'd just gotten what I considered positive news and had a prudent plan. Kristen's tone made me defensive, but this being the first day of the new Palmieri Age of Tranquility, I didn't argue. And anyway, I had a busy week ahead, and that's what I wanted to think about.

"Okay, we'll look into it," I said.

"I'll call today," she said.

"Well, hold on. Do we want Anna to miss more school and dance? We're already taking her out for another day with the NYU appointment."

No answer.

"Let's wait until after the recital," I continued. "Then we'll meet with whomever you want."

"It's not my *wanting* to, like it's for me. It's the smart thing to do," she said.

"Thank you for guiding me to the *smart* thing to do," I said. "What would I do without you, Kristen?"

The tranquility campaign had hardly launched, and here we were.

"Don't be sarcastic," she said.

"I'm just thinking about school and dance, and you're not. The recital's only in a month or something."

"I've been a teacher over twenty years and danced for my entire youth," she shot back. "Believe me, I'm thinking about school and dance."

Exit Kristen, stage right.

As the start of baseball always meant spring to me, the Robert Mann Dance Center's annual dance recital had come to mean summer to all of us. Right around Memorial Day, there'd be the jazz, tap, lyrical, ballet, modern, and hip-hop dance extravaganza in a packed local college auditorium. Here, the ten-month-long, five-day-a-week afternoon and evening studio class regimen would come to a grand finale. It was the big show; the glimmering, rollicking payoff for everyone's hard work. Thanks to the panic attacks, Anna had now missed not only a competition but also Monday's company rehearsal. We were getting close enough to recital time that I figured this suggestion to Kristen about missing anything more would land well. Dance was Kristen's world. Even if I did think a new doctor's opinion was important, I couldn't imagine fitting in another item of any kind on our schedule until June, when softball, the recital, the girls' school year, Kristen's school year, and my semester would all be over. After she left, with our disagreement unresolved, Kristen reentered the room. In the theatre, this is known as a "false exit."

"I don't want to wait," she said. "We're calling today."

"It's not *waiting*," I barked back. "Don't try to make it sound like I'm putting something off. It's called *being reasonable*."

Of course, she was right. And I was far from being reasonable. A new doctor might find something else. And that's what

I was afraid of. I took a deep breath in through my nose and out through my mouth.

The social worker at the hospital had given us all a lesson in deep breathing, explaining how it's a way of gaining control of any moment where panic might try to take hold. When we'd gotten home from Cohen's, we all practiced together. The point was to help Anna, but our marriage could sure use it too.

"Have a nice day," I said to Kristen.

"You too," she said. "I'll call them and let you know when the appointment will be."

I didn't reply. At this point I couldn't even fit arguing into my schedule. The last few days of hospital isolation had thrown me out of my already tight routine, and I was way behind on classwork.

I was on track to finish a strong rookie year at Mercy. My superiors seemed happy with my performance, I'd published some short essays in anthologies, made my way onto a couple school committees, and advised the theatre club. A good start, I thought. Further, this would be a very different end of an academic year for me. Until now, the big dance recital, aside from being the unofficial beginning of summer, was also the official beginning of my even-more-strict-than-usual financial austerity, the annual three-month stop of regular paychecks. As any adjunct knows, once a semester ends, the pay ends, and the already-tight belt would get tighter. But now, as a full timer, I would get paid all through summer break. I imagined I'd feel like a rich man compared with what I was used to.

I was scooping the eggs onto plates.

"I don't want to go to school today," I heard Anna say behind me. I turned around. She was still in her pajamas.

"Anna, you have to. You can't fall behind any more than you already have. You know that."

"I'm scared," she said, then shook once, as if a chill ran through her. "What if it happens at school?"

"The doctor says it won't," I said. "So did the social worker. And if you feel something, you know what to do."

"Yeah, whatever. Breathe deep," she said snidely. "In through the mouth, out through the nose."

"I think it's the other way around."

Anna was clearly not consoled, but she started to eat. I gave her the Lacosamide at its morning dose, a 5mg dose of Clobazam, which I'd picked up at the pharmacy the day before, then the CBD oil. With this, I realized I hadn't updated another of Anna's doctors on all that happened over the weekend. She was the MD we'd see for the medical marijuana.

"Keep thinking of things that relax you," I said, doing my best to keep the atmosphere positive. "Happy things. Think of the dance recital. It's coming up! And think of Rhode Island! Happy Fourth!"

"I can't wait to see my cousins," Anna said, and smiled a little.

My brother Scott was a bit like me. A few years younger, he was more established in his career. A former college ballplayer turned writer and professor, he was also a veteran chair of the English department at Johnson & Wales University with a PhD. He and his wife Christine had three kids, and Anna and Nora were never happier than when they were with them. Christine was a registered nurse, and when Kristen called her, she didn't contradict what the Cohen's people said about girls that were Anna's age and panic attacks. She had seen many such cases.

Anna slowly ate. I noticed something looked different about her. Her brow was furrowed. She had the face of an older person.

"I'll be looking for a nice therapist to help you with stuff," I said. "You can talk about anything bothering you. Anything at all."

"Will he yell at me?"

"God, no!" I said. "And it doesn't have to be a 'he,' of course."

"I want the scary thoughts to go away," she said, and another jumpy chill shook her. "And the seizures too. Can he do that? Or *she*?"

I kept up my super-positive voice.

"We're gonna figure it out. All of it."

"So that's a 'no,'" Anna said.

"Daddy?" Nora entered the kitchen. As usual, without the slightest assistance, she was showered and dressed, with her schoolbag packed and bed made.

"Morning, Nora."

"I got a one hundred and two on my math test."

"That's awesome, Nora."

Of course, I should have said more. I should have showered her with grateful praise, as if this delightful little kid just made my day. By now, it was as if I only knew how to half engage with things that weren't intense threats. Nora reported good news as she usually did about her schoolwork, and I may as well have simply said, "Thanks for not making things worse, Nora."

"You have to sign it," Nora added.

"I'm proud to sign it," I said. "A one hundred!"

"One hundred and two," she said.

I dropped both girls at their schools, then headed to my office in Dobbs Ferry. I had a few hours until class but beforehand, some essay grading, prepping the remaining lectures of the week, answering emails, and organizing a tech rehearsal plan for the theatre club.

As I made my way over the Throgs Neck Bridge and into Westchester, I made some calls. I felt I needed to report to Anna's school what had happened over the weekend, why she missed Monday, and the new diagnosis. I left a message with the assistant principal, Mrs. Kelly, who had helped me from the start with Anna's accommodations in her ICT class.

Since she entered middle school, it had taken numerous conversations, meetings, emails, and letters from doctors to get the teachers to reasonably adhere to what was stipulated in her Individualized Education Plan. An IEP is a personalized set of academic support modifications and adjustments for children who suffer from a disability, attention issue, learning disorder, or anything that might be an obstacle to their keeping up with the mainstream curriculum. The elementary school Anna had attended was very good with all this, but now, it sometimes seemed like some of the middle school teachers hadn't even read Anna's IEP. Middle school teachers have a lot on their plate; a larger number of students to keep track of. My mother was a middle school teacher and always said it's the hardest kind of teaching there is. I don't deny it. Add to the already-difficult environment, the usual lack of funding, and any number of kids' very detailed and custom IEPs, it must seem nearly impossible.

Epilepsy can be a tricky thing for teachers. First, until a seizure hits, it's completely hidden. It doesn't come with crutches, a wheelchair, thick-lensed glasses, a palsied limb, or whatever else so many pained parents send their children into the system with. Anna, who might be in a zombie-like state for any number of reasons related to her condition, could look like any other half-dazed sixth grader at her desk and not someone who needed assistance discerning, for example, which line on a map of the Louisiana Purchase intersected with the other, because her eyes were jumping all over the page, and her forehead felt like it was being hit with a hammer.

Mrs. Kelly called me right back and said she would let the teachers know about this new anxiety diagnosis, as well as alert the paraprofessional, Ms. Lee, who was assigned to keep eyes on Anna all day. I wasn't exactly sure what I was asking them all to do at this point. "Ask everyone to go easy on Anna, she has a panic disorder" felt like an inappropriate request, but I figured it was better they knew. My next call was to the school nurse, who echoed what my sister-in-law and the social worker at Cohen's told us.

"We hear about this a lot," the nurse said, sympathetically. "This is the age where lots of drama starts. Kids get mean. They feel pressure about grades. Anna's already been through so much. Poor baby."

I liked the school nurse, and it felt like she had a soft spot for Anna and for us. Her own daughter, now fully grown, had grown up with a seizure disorder. It was a far milder case than Anna's, but she knew well how it could rock a household over the years.

"Anna's always so happy looking," she said. "She dances in the halls."

"Thank you," I said.

"I'll check on her throughout the day."

"We learned some deep breathing methods. That's what she's supposed to do if she starts feeling things."

"Good," the nurse said. "I'll remind her."

Then, for what was left of the forty-five-minute drive to the bucolic Hudson riverside campus on this cool sunny morning, there was quiet. No radio, no music; just the sound of my car cutting through the wind. With every few minutes that passed without a call from the middle school, I began allowing myself to think more about things other than epilepsy, or whatever else about Anna's life that made my stomach feel like there were bullets in it.

I thought of my plans for the day's Understanding Movies class. I thought of my old roommate Michael, now a very successful television actor and scheduled to soon be a guest to my Play Directing class. I thought about my travel baseball team's first practice coming in a couple weeks. It was a relief to start catching up on things mentally.

I made it to Mercy in just under an hour. I parked the car, got a coffee from the dining hall, and decided to take a walk. The campus was glowing. In the sweet breeze off the river, I could hear the shouts and whistles of the early lacrosse practice on the athletic fields that run along the Hudson beyond Main Hall. Across a meadow toward where my office is, in Victory Hall, I saw a groundskeeper on a small tractor dragging the infield dirt of the softball field. Must be a game today, I thought. Perfect weather for it. I saw students pass in pajama pants and sweatshirts, walking from the dorms to get breakfast. Another student wearing headphones was reading on a bench.

I loved to walk around and picture my daughters as students someday. If I ever had anything to do with getting them there, it would mean that the long jumble of my creative life that somehow qualified me to teach had become worth something. There I'd picture myself, years from now, along one of the paths between buildings, holding some kind of briefcase, on my way to my office maybe. I'd hear Anna or Nora, or maybe both, call to me. I'd look up and see them, on their way somewhere, like back to the dorms after breakfast, healthy and happy.

I got to my office. Jay, Communication Studies program director, was just leaving.

"How you doin'?" he said.

"Great. You?"

"Baseball weather," he said. "Feel like putting on the uniform?"

"Of course," I said.

"Team can use you."

The baseball team had been slumping. I laughed. I told him I'd think about it. I realized how normal I sounded, just a guy passing by his colleague exchanging a little charm on a nice, sunny, normal day. As I sat in my chair, I considered telling Jay what happened over the weekend. He was easy to talk to and funny as hell. We were hired together and had been friends from the first day of faculty orientation. Maybe it would have been healthy to unload it on him, but, as usual, I resisted. I always had the instinct to avoid burdening people with the horrific stories of Anna's condition, which also spared myself from having to relive them.

Jay headed for his class, and I started organizing my desk for a few minutes, and there it came—the cell phone. I looked at the number. The middle school. My heart did its usual tingling shrink and I felt the adrenaline pump through me. I took a breath and answered, ready to face whatever had happened. It wasn't even 10 a.m.

"Hello Mr. Palmieri, it's Mary, the School Nurse at M.S. 158," the voice said.

"Hello," I said. So much for what they said about this not happening at school, I thought. "I guess we didn't last long."

"Anna's been to see me twice." I dropped my head on the desk. "The first time was just a few minutes after we spoke this morning. She said she was feeling things in class and was scared.

We sat and talked, and she seemed to calm down. I asked her if she wanted me to call you, but she said she'd try to go back. Then she came again."

"She's with you now?"

"She's with Mrs. Kelly," the nurse said. "They're deep breathing in the hall."

As William Blake wrote, excessive sorrow laughs. There was nothing comical about this in any way, and, in fact, I was touched by what the nurse had just told me. Despite everything, the image of this executive school administrator heaving and blowing with Anna in the hallway made me want to laugh. It was all so dreary and ridiculous, it reminded me instantly of not only my stethoscope folly, but of another misadventure: our "train your own seizure dog" experiment.

Anna was eight or nine at the time. We had been looking into service dog possibilities. The process of obtaining one is long and rigorous and in most ways not fit for the particulars of Anna's case. Epilepsy service dogs are trained to respond to their person's seizures. The dog will bark and circle them when they hit, increasing the chances that someone intervenes to help. The dog is trained from a very early age, and the partnership with the human takes months to build. People suggested we get Anna on one of the long waitlists for these programs, but we didn't see it as something that would have made much of a difference in her life. Anna was always in her bed when she would seize, and we knew where she was and what we had to do. There was no real point in having her feel any more different out in public than she already did by having a red-and-white-vested service dog at her side everywhere she went.

We had heard stories, though, of dogs who were able to detect seizures *before* the person had them—as if they could sense it or smell one coming. They would begin to bark wildly to communicate to the person to sit down somewhere safe and get ready. If such a thing was true, we thought, maybe we could find a dog who would enable us to let Anna sleep alone. We'd already tried baby cams, movement detectors; even a wristband that was supposed to signal an oncoming seizure by noting a change of heart rate. None of these worked. Now, we imagined a handsome hero dog downstairs with us, ears shooting up, barking, racing up to Anna's room, knowing that a seizure was coming.

We knew this magical talent was an irregular biproduct of service dogs' training; not what they were deliberately trained for. The animals somehow learned it on their own. But we read about another related benefit of getting a dog. Statistics showed that epilepsy patients who had dogs tended to have less stress, and therefore fewer seizures. So, we got a "Yorkie-poo": half Miniature Poodle, half Yorkshire Terrier, both of which we read were among the breeds that had been known to pick up this magical sixth sense.

Rosalind became a beloved pet, but never once did she predict or even respond with any interest to one of Anna's seizures. My attempt to train her as a service dog was the comic memory I had while picturing Mrs. Kelly. For months, when Ros was a puppy, I would, as usual, respond to Anna's seizures with my same emergency protocol. I'd climb onto her bed, hold her arms away from her face and windpipe, pin the legs down, etc. For the first year of Ros's tenure in the house, though, I'd do all this and bark too. I hoped she would take my performance as a demonstration of her future responsibilities. The puppy, if she even woke up at all, would watch me with total indifference. I wondered sometimes if the neighbors heard me, and what they thought was going on in our house.

Mrs. Kelly came to the phone. She told me she had gotten the word out about Anna's weekend to the teachers and that Ms. Lee had brought Anna to the nurse, having noticed she seemed distressed. Anna asked to speak with me.

"Daddy, I want to come home."

"Anna, I need you to try to—"

"Pick me up please."

"I'm not close to home right now. I'm at the college."

"I'll wait in the nurse's office."

"Anna," I said, ramping up the authority, "I need you to get through this."

"I'm scared. I felt like I was falling."

"That's okay. You know you're not."

"Come pick me up."

"You can't miss your classes, honey."

"Pick me up."

"Anna, if you have to miss school, you'll have to miss dance." Silence.

"Why?" she said.

Tuesday was her one school day without dance class, so this was a bit of a bluff on my part.

"Because if you're not well enough for—"

"That's dumb," she said.

"Anna."

"What?" she said angrily. "You're forcing me!"

"I need you to try," I said.

Another silence.

"Anna?"

"I felt like I was falling off a cliff," she said. It was clear she was crying now. "Why is this happening?"

"You mean...like your breathing feels like that? What do you mean?" I said.

"I see it. I'm on the edge of a cliff, and I fall over."

I didn't know if she was saying what she meant, that she was describing a feeling of some kind, or she was actually seeing herself on an actual cliff.

"You mean you close your eyes and see this?"

"No. It just comes."

"So you *see* a cliff and go over it?"

"Almost."

I had nothing left. I couldn't bring myself to get the nurse or assistant principal back on the phone to tell them that my sixth grader was hallucinating, or unable to clearly explain what she was experiencing. It made me sick, but I kept pushing her. They seemed so confident discharging us at the hospital.

"Anna, return to class and deal with it. I'll pick you up after school."

She hung up. I felt awful and nearly called right back, but I remembered that I wanted to update the medical marijuana doctor. I had forgotten her full name (we'd only seen her twice), so I typed into the search engine the words: *medical marijuana children doctor Westchester epilepsy.*

Dr. Junella Chin's website appeared first, with her authored articles filling the screen beneath, but at the bottom I noticed something else under the "Related Searches" list: *Marijuana Overdose.*

I clicked that link and now running down the screen were essays, studies, testimonials, and warnings about cannabis side effects. I read one, then another, then another, and in each, I found every symptom we'd seen for the last seventy-two hours:

escalated heart rate, headache, pale skin, paranoid thoughts, hallucination, and...panic attacks.

And just like that, I felt we were as lost as when it all began, wondering just how bad things would get, and if we would ever really know what to do, when one doctor's opinion might be contradicted by the next, one diagnosis replaced with another. After seven years of the seizures having a relative consistency being nocturnal, we'd normalized, even accepted, living with them. Still, with each new medicine Anna was put on, like medical marijuana, there was an undeniable hope it would prove the silver bullet. But they'd all been failures. And some had been poison.

CHAPTER FOUR

LOVE AND LABOR

When Anna was put on her first seizure medications, it was explained to us that they often have what's called a "Honeymoon Period," wherein they work for some time before proving ineffective. I suppose it's a good term for any time in life where you think things are going a good way, but they're actually not, and you just don't know it yet.

Our very first months with Anna were everything new parents would have hoped for. Kristen was on maternity leave. She had "banked" enough unused sick days over the years to be paid through a few months at home, during which we were covered by my Screen Actors Guild health plan. Family and friends would come and visit us in our two-bedroom Astoria rental. Mother and baby took long, lovely walks on the neighborhood streets and in the park along the Queens side bank of the East River. Sometimes, elderly neighborhood Greek gentlemen would tuck money into the stroller. I wondered if this was tradition, or if they knew the baby's dad was Marc Palmieri and that she would need it.

At the pediatrician, Anna met every one of her developmental "milestones." She was an engaging baby with a long attention span. She belly laughed a lot, not only when we were trying to make her laugh, but at things she found funny on her own—like the cracking of eggs, the sound of a toilet flushing, or the voice from the Rosetta Stone French lessons I was failing at for the third or fourth time in my life.

I was thirty and Kristen was twenty-nine when we got married. For kids, the plan was to wait five years. Until then, we would enjoy everything about living as lovers in New York City, take some trips, be with our family and friends, put money away, and do whatever else we felt like.

Professionally, we had plans too. Kristen would continue teaching at the elementary school on Long Island she'd worked for since graduating from SUNY Oneonta. She loved her students and colleagues and was continuing to take courses to reach sixty "continuing ed" credits beyond her master's in special education. Once she completed those, her salary would be lifted to the top of her union pay scale, the next benchmark in an already successful career.

My plan was to actually have a career. To me, that meant making enough money at things I wanted to do, not relying on the kind of survival jobs I'd had since the first days I lived in the city.

My first professional goal had been to be a baseball player, but now it was to be a writer and actor. None of these could be called safe career aspirations. Very few people get to make a living as an athlete or an artist. I never even really got started with pro baseball. At eighteen, as a senior in high school, I turned down the Blue Jays offer to accept a scholarship to Wake Forest University with every expectation I'd be drafted again after college. Wake was in one of the best athletic conferences in the NCAA and I more than held my own. My final game my senior year in college,

I beat Miami, throwing eighty-eight miles an hour all the way into the last inning. A Padres scout in the stands that day was one of a number of scouts who told my coaches they'd be submitting my name for the draft.

But the 1993 MLB draft came and went, and my name never came up. It was a heartbreak, my first major failure, but rather than taking the risk of prolonging the heartbreak in chasing free agency and open tryouts, a route that landed a few of my friends in the minor leagues, I walked away. I went back to Wake to complete my degree in communications. The previous fall, I'd seen my first ever "straight" play, the department's production of Tennessee Williams's *The Night of the Iguana*, and it blew me away. I knew right then that if baseball ever had to end, which of course it did, there'd be another dream to take its place.

I started with an acting class, then got cast in some student plays. I loved it so much, I cobbled together a minor in theatre, and made the plan to move to New York City to be an actor. When you decide to pursue a dream like that, you commit to existing on part-time or even full-time "survival" jobs, and that had been the life I'd come to lead when Kristen and I reconnected for our fateful coffee date.

By the time we were having our little reunion, I'd managed to do a few visible showbiz things, like the soaps, commercials, and getting my name and picture in movie and play reviews in *Variety* and the *New York Times*, but nothing was as consistent money-wise as the job at the insurance agency, the typist gig, and coaching. Those jobs were depressing me at that point, not because they were hard, or the people weren't nice, or I didn't love being out on the field, but because they had nothing to do with what I came to the city for.

Six years later, when Kristen gave birth to Anna in 2006, I still had all my many jobs, but I was very close to making just enough to exist purely as an artist. I'd begun to be regularly cast in union contract stage productions each year at the Axis Company. I was booking more commercials. My agent in LA was negotiating my second screenplay option. My play, *Levittown*, the one that opened the week Anna came into the world, was about to come out in its published form, and every six months, a bit of royalty money trickled in from book sales and performances of my previous plays. I'd taught an acting class at a community college in New Jersey and just accepted the playwriting course at City College.

I felt like I had eggs in better baskets. Our old plans were coming together. Kristen would enjoy her maternity leave, then when she'd go back to work, I'd drop the jobs I didn't want to do and stay home with the baby. If I had an audition, I'd bring Baby with me. I'd seen actors do this all the time. If I had a class to teach, I'd hire a sitter to watch her on campus. I'd write while Baby slept, play with Baby when awake, then hand Baby off to Kristen when she'd get home. I'd be out the door heading for the theatre or an evening class to teach. It would be the hustling household of Palmieris. Baby, schoolteacher, and working artist.

This meant a lot to me. Becoming a parent had only intensified my need to feel successful. I couldn't look at myself as a legitimate writer, actor, or professor while I was still relying on other jobs. I wanted to be fully "one thing" rather than partially many things. Of course, most people in the arts have to sustain themselves with other employment, and when I was with my friends, most of whom were in the same boat, I never felt shame in it. But outside those circles, it didn't feel so honorable. Everybody else seemed to know what they were: an identifiable, professionally speaking, "one thing." My parents, siblings, and in-laws were "one thing." Neighbors were "one thing." Old college and high school friends were thriving at their "one thing." They were sales reps, chiropractors, construction workers, contractors, actuaries, architects, managers, accountants, lawyers...they had predictable workweeks, vacation days, retirement plans, property, and gainful incomes. This was why I always hated "What do you do, Marc?" If I only answered with the work I was proud of, I felt like a fraud.

During Anna's first months, I usually left the apartment before she and Kristen were awake and came home after they'd gone to sleep. Every day was an odyssey, sometimes hitting both the insurance and periodontist offices, a class, an audition, and either a rehearsal if I was in a play or a baseball practice if we were in season. I looked forward to the time I'd be able to have not only with the baby once Kristen returned to her job and our roles swapped, but also to more time for my own creative work. I couldn't possibly write more scripts when every day I had to crisscross the city and beyond.

I had my handful of scrapes with success over the years, but each time, I worried that would be the last of it. I seemed to be living in a pattern that started long ago, with baseball. I was sure I'd get another chance after I turned that first contract down. Instead, I'd see college teammates and opponents make the big leagues. In college, I beat out future all-stars, was on pitching staffs with future World Series winners, but now, I was a high school coach. Kevin Jarvis and Mike Buddie, both fellow pitchers at Wake, made it all the way up with the Reds and Yankees, respectively. I once struck out Jason Varitek, who'd go on to become a member of the Boston Red Sox Hall of Fame. Another former teammate, Ross Atkins, played in the minors and eventually became a Major

League general manager. Now, my years as an artist were starting to feel like they'd end as baseball had: a promising start, ending in nothing. I'd written a movie with big stars in it, and my life hardly changed. A year later, I optioned a television pilot to a major Hollywood production company, but it was never produced. I'd spent a pilot season in Los Angeles when *Too Much Sleep* was up for a Spirit Award but got very few auditions. My plays got good reviews, but I couldn't quite get to the next level.

Meanwhile, peers were progressing. My old roommates, for instance. Michael made it to Broadway. George was getting damn close. Thomas Kail, who, while having a survival job of his own, had directed my *Levittown* for a festival downtown, then went on to direct the Tony-winning *In the Heights* (then *Hamilton* after that). I was watching people I worked closely with grow more successful, some making it big—and each time, while I was happy for them, it hurt a little too. It could feel like I was destined to be left behind.

It was Anna's fifth month, just days before Kristen would be back at her job. Days away from the next phase in raising our child together in the city. My life's recurring almost-but-not-quite motif felt it was ending. Soon, I'd be able to write, act, and teach for a living. I wouldn't exactly be "one thing," but I felt this would be even better.

Kristen too was eager for the change. As heavenly as these months had been with her little partner, she was the first to admit that much more time out of work would drive her insane. And she had her own plan afoot: to work another two years, then have baby number two.

I gave my two-week notice at both office jobs. I'd be out by Thanksgiving.

Then came November 13, 2006. Life became NewYork-Presbyterian Hospital's Pediatric Intensive Care Unit, a place where parents like us wept and howled in the halls. Like us, they'd found that all that time making plans for their lives, for their children, had been a kind of honeymoon period: wonderful while it lasted, but over now, gone, and a bit harder to remember, as every new day came.

＊

November 13, 2006. Our apartment's living room. Anna was in her bouncy seat. Kristen noticed that now and then, as she made noises and played, she'd stop for a moment, go silent, her eyes seeming blank. She called the pediatrician and described what she was seeing. He told her it sounded like seizures, and to drive Anna immediately to NewYork-Presbyterian.

I met the car a few avenues from the hospital. Anna was in her car seat in the back. I sat beside her. Within a few moments, I saw her seize for the first time. Kristen and I said very little, other than who would park the car and who would run in with the baby.

The rooms and hallways of the pediatric ER at NewYork-Presbyterian had walls like one would see in a nursery school. Bright, colorful painted scenes of blue skies, cotton-white clouds, green grassy hills, playful animals, and cartoon characters. Anna's seizures continued and became longer. By Kristen's count, she had about twenty of them since they left the apartment, some lasting nearly a minute.

A young resident saw us first, while a nurse took blood pressure. Anna was crying harder than I'd ever heard her. We were told she would likely have brain scans within the hour, so she couldn't eat or drink, because general anesthesia might be needed to keep her still. Kristen knew the baby was painfully hungry and thirsty, but all she could do was hold her. The cries were constant. They were sounds of a raw surprise and anger. There beside her on the bed was her mother, the source of all sustenance, holding her, but refusing her.

The nurse started a blood draw from a vein in Anna's inner arm, and the crying became all-out wailing. I felt myself turn off like a tripped machine. Kristen never stopped whispering into Anna's ears, over and over.

"I know. Mommy's here. I love you. I know."

The on-call neurologist arrived.

"What happened here, my beautiful baby?" she said, soft-spoken with a British accent.

She asked us to tell her everything, everything we'd seen of the seizures and anything else that seemed out of the ordinary in Anna's delivery or first months of life. Before today, as far as we knew, nothing had been out of the ordinary. We said so, and just as Kristen began describing the seizures, Anna went into another one. The doctor watched it happen closely as Kristen held her through it, then ordered a dose of Phenobarbital. She told us that once this calmed her down, Anna would be taken for a CT scan.

Calming her down took longer than expected. The first dose didn't seem to have an effect. Anna sobbed painfully for near five-minute intervals until another seizure hit, silencing her, now lasting up to a minute and a half. Her eyes would go vacant, her right arm would rise, and she'd slowly lean to her left, as if about to roll over in slow motion. Then, she'd seem to jolt out of it, surprised, as if having been shaken from sleep, then cry again. After a half hour, they gave another Phenobarb dose. It failed to sedate her completely, but by then, she seemed so spent that she'd fall asleep. The five-minute gaps between seizures became more like twenty minutes.

Within an hour, they brought her out of the room, leaving Kristen and me in silence.

"Did you call your parents?" she asked, after a few minutes.

"No."

It was 2006, before text messaging was my main means of communication. My little phone at the time could have probably done it, but I never used it that way, nor would our parents have had any idea how to receive a text. Calling meant calling, and the only person I'd reached out to so far was the Axis Company stage manager. I had told him something was up with the baby and that it was possible I'd be late that night to rehearsal. I was in the company's annual holiday children's play, which still had a few weeks before opening. Something stopped me from saying anything to him about "seizures."

"Can you please call your parents?" Kristen said. "And mine?"

I didn't want to. Not yet. Maybe whatever held me back on details with the stage manager was also holding me back from calling our parents. Just as with Jay in my office years later, I couldn't bring myself to start spreading the fear we were experiencing among our peers and loved ones. Maybe I felt this would all be solved and over within a few hours. Just a passing scare. Wasn't this what parenthood was famous for anyway? Passing scares, false alarms, terrifying moments to tell the kids about later in life? So why whip everyone up?

"Let's see what they say after the scan," I said.

"Please call," she said, sternly.

I looked at my phone. No signal. This part of the ER was deep in the building.

"Sorry," I said. "No signal, and I really don't think I can bring myself to leave this room until they come back and tell us what they see on that scan."

I tried to keep the faith that they would see absolutely nothing bad, that this was the result of some light infection, something we'd flush out with some water, rest, or antibiotic. It may have been two hours before the doctor returned.

"We got the CT. There seems to be some brain asymmetry, but that could be because she moved slightly while taking it," she explained. The "asymmetry" was a staggering thing to hear, despite the potential explanation. "The seizure cluster is persisting, and we need to get it stopped. We are adding more Phenobarbital intravenously and will admit her upstairs. They're preparing the bed. Let's get her stabilized and see what's causing this, okay Mom and Dad?"

"So the scan is good news?" Kristen said.

"Well, assuming the asymmetry was caused by movement, it didn't reveal any clear abnormalities," the doctor said. "But the seizures are continuing, so let's keep looking."

This sounded like a dodge or at least a very measured answer. I didn't see anything positive in it, but Kristen seemed to. I felt at that moment as if I'd noticed something in what the doctor said that Kristen didn't, and my heart hurt for her. I had no idea what exactly to make of this brain "asymmetry" comment. I'd pictured something lopsided, or something important on one side that wasn't on the other. I was too scared to ask the doctor what else this could mean. It opened up a new world of things to imagine now, including the possibility that something was gravely wrong with our child. I looked over at Kristen, who had closed her eyes in exhaustion. Her arms, which had just been holding Anna, were now empty. Only months ago, with the baby still in her womb,

Kristen would write letters, telling her she loved her already and would take care of her forever.

I myself had wanted so many things from life. Kristen had wanted Anna—and there, I had the thought that she would never have her alive in those arms again, that the "forever" in those letters would turn out to be five and a half months. An emotion I thought would overcome me began to swell. I told Kristen I'd go outside to call our parents to calmly let them know where we were and why.

When I reached the lobby, my legs weren't ready to stop, so I kept walking. Fast. I exited the hospital, walked along the entrance driveway circle, up the street past York Avenue and all the way to First. I looked around at the cars, trucks, and people walking this way and that and thought how odd it felt that none of them knew the slightest thing about what was happening just two avenues away. I felt as if they couldn't possibly fail to notice as they passed me, this man on the corner in deep distress, facing the possibility of the ultimate human pain. I turned back and saw the hospital in the short distance, towering into the southern sky, and wondered for a moment how many people like me have stood right here, gazing in dismay at that building, facing a catastrophe.

I headed back, and when I was near the ER again, I saw benches. Nearly breathless, I sat and called my father, wondering where he was on this routine Monday, about to have it turned upside down. When he answered, I told him Anna was having seizures, that we didn't know why, that they had not yet been stopped, and that she was being admitted into intensive care. I could detect a rattling in his voice as he asked me which hospital. He then told me he was halfway to a meeting in Philly, but was now turning around to come straight over and would call my mother.

We walked behind Anna's bed as they slowly wheeled her onto the PICU floor. She was deeply sedated but still seizing now and then, mostly noticeable by her arm stiffening. She had an IV stuck into the top of her tiny hand, and a pulse monitor on a toe. When we got to our corner, the technicians plugged in all the wires and set up standing screens. As they started to attach the twelve or so electrodes to her scalp, Anna sprung fully awake. This process was even more harrowing than the blood test, which they'd done after a third dose of Phenobarb. That was all bad enough, but when the electrode leads were being glued on, she screamed bloody murder.

When everything was fastened, they stretched a small, white gauze hat over Anna's head, and fastened padded guardrails to the bedsides. She seemed to have exhausted herself, struggling to open her eyes when we spoke to her. A seizure poked through only once every hour or so now, and when that happened, the machines that stood behind and beside her bed would chime loud with alarms.

It felt like we'd reached some kind of plateau. There were wires attached all over her body, but we were told she wouldn't be plugged in here for long, as they'd need to move her for more tests. The doctors spoke to our pediatrician on the phone, and a spinal tap was ordered, followed by an MRI. They explained again that they'd need her to be completely still, and because an occasional seizure was still breaking through, she'd go under the general anesthesia this time and be intubated. We signed papers, and they took her away.

Through the huge windows of the PICU floor, we could see that it was nearing sunset. Coast Guard patrol boats, long flat barges, and the occasional tour boat sailed by on the East River below us. My father had already gone and returned again from Long Island with my mother. Kristen's parents were there. The wait for a doctor to update us was excruciating. Our parents all had questions, but we had no answers other than what we'd seen, and so far been told, which wasn't much. It'd been hours since I looked at my phone, and I realized I never followed up with the stage manager. I had missed a call from Randy, the Axis Company artistic director, and went out to the floor elevator bank to call her back. What I saw on my walk out, all of which I missed on the way in, so focused on Anna, were the saddest sights I'd seen in my life. I had never been in a place like this.

Like the ER, the walls had a bright, cheery décor—mostly New York City-themed. One hall was Central Park, another had the New York sports teams, another had skyscrapers and the Statue of Liberty, and yet another was decorated like Times Square. Along these walls, though, were live tableaus of utter suffering. Couples embraced just outside the doorways to their children's rooms, barely standing, holding each other up. Passing the other PICU rooms, I saw kids of all ages and sizes in the beds, some awake, some unconscious, laid out under tubes and pumps. There were children with severe physical deformities, and there were others, like Anna, showing no outward sign of anything amiss, but who lay there, motionless. The sounds of the place were computer chirps, respirator gasps, beeps, phones ringing, and pager calls. And crying, everywhere. Doctors, nurses, technicians, and people who looked like parents or other family walked with grim expressions this way and that.

I had been regularly working for Randy Sharp at Axis for a couple years. She was the artistic director who also wrote shows, composed music, and was about the most charismatic human being I knew. Hyperintelligent, studious, curious, and eternally cynical about the New York Theatre world, she was among its most prolific producers. She knew a thing about resiliency. That's the word she told me to hold onto as we spoke on the phone.

"Marc, listen to me. Children's brains are resilient," she said. I was standing in the hall near the elevators, having caught her up on the day we'd had. "Children are strong. Please remember that. They're stronger than us."

She was telling me to hold on to this, no matter what they found on these scans. I told her I was sorry to miss rehearsal. She said who the hell cares. I said I still hoped this would come to a happy, quick resolution and that I'd see her tomorrow.

A resolution, of sorts, did come, but not very quickly. We were in the PICU for nearly a week. The seizure clusters were suppressed completely by day three, with so much Phenobarb that Anna could no longer sit up. She slept most of the time, awake only to moan and twist during the blood tests that came twice a day to measure the drug levels in her blood, or when they had to reglue an EEG electrode that came loose.

The spinal tap was negative. It wasn't meningitis, and the first read on the MRI was inconclusive, like the CT scan, but more doctors and radiologists conferred over the films as the days continued.

"They're reviewing it all again tomorrow," the floor pediatrician told us on day four. "Fingers crossed. If they declare the MRI is all clear…." He stopped there but made a face and gesture that said, "Then there's a bottom to all this, and we'll get her right."

Kristen was breastfeeding Anna, so she slept each night on the cot in our section of the floor, and she never stepped away much longer than for the shower and bathroom in the PICU hall. Family from both our sides was there every day, morning to night. I came and went. Between however many daily hours at the hospital, I managed to get uptown for my class and stopped by the periodontists' office to clear the work that had backed up for days. At night, I slept at home in our apartment, but I was never alone. George, who was also in rehearsals for the show at Axis, stayed over.

George was worried about me. I could tell. Each night at my apartment, he insisted I have as many beers as I liked, until I could fall asleep. If my cell phone rang with a call from Kristen that said I needed to come speeding to the hospital, a sober George would be behind the wheel.

I talked a lot, and George mainly listened. I tried to avoid stating the obvious, that I was in a general state of mental and emotional arrest. We managed to talk a bit about the thing we loved to do together, which was theatre. It had occurred to me that on the day all of this started, when I got that call from Kristen, it was Shakespeare's play *Love's Labour's Lost* I'd just referred to in my class. I found it funny, I told George. *Love's Labour's* happened to be the first play he ever saw me do in New York City, years before, in a church on the Upper West Side. Even more fitting for how that happy day in the classroom would end up turning out was that it's the one romantic comedy of Shakespeare's that, right at the end, takes a major turn into darkness. A messenger arrives, announcing that the king is dead, and his daughter, the romantic lead, heads into mourning. The lovers part, sad songs are sung, and...end of play.

The next morning, when George and I arrived back at the PICU, a large group of doctors and neuroradiologists, most of whom I had not seen before, was already in the room. One seemed to have just finished explaining something to everyone. The first person I saw was my mother.

"Mom?" I said.

"They found something," she said softly.

I noticed George stepping behind me. I felt my body want to go into tantrum mode, even though I didn't yet know what they'd found. Whatever it was, I knew my mother's face was sad.

"Okay, what is it?" I said. The neurologist who had been overseeing the case, Dr. Sabiha Merchant, stepped into my view, approaching me.

"Mr. Palmieri," she said to me.

"Yes."

"It was obscure on the films, difficult to pinpoint at first, but we are confident now," she said. "Anna has a malformation of the left frontal lobe."

She led me to a monitor with a brain image on the screen. She ran her finger around a small oval-shaped area that was slightly darker than what was around it.

"What is it?" I said.

"We call it cortical dysplasia. A brain lesion."

"Okay," I said.

"It was formed in utero, sometime in the first trimester," Dr. Merchant explained. "It's grey matter tissue that never unfolded like it was supposed to."

"What does that mean? What do I do?"

I wanted information fast. Mainly, I wanted to know if this meant that Anna would die. I looked toward Anna's bed for Kristen. There were too many people in the room. I couldn't find her.

"The good news is," continued the doctor. "There seems to be no other issues with the brain, and nothing looks damaged by the seizures. And the area of the defect does not control learning, language, or motor skills."

"That's all good!" I said.

"Yes," she said. "She can have a normal life but will have to stay on medication."

"Treatable," I said. I was beginning to feel a comeback in my legs, arms, and heartbeat. "Some medicine. That's what it'll be?"

So what? I thought to myself. Pop a pill and live your life. If only everyone on this floor would get news like this. I turned and hugged my mother. I saw George watching me. I gave him a thumbs up. He gave it back.

"This isn't bad, Mom," I said. "Right? It's treatable. They'll give her medicine. We're lucky."

"Yes," my mother said, but she didn't mean it.

The doctors said Anna would now be put on a medication called Oxcarbazepine, and the Phenobarbital would be weaned over months. We'd follow up for long-term care with Dr. Gail Solomon, a veteran neurologist who worked with Dr. Merchant.

The previous few days had been terrible, but now that we had our diagnosis, it didn't take long for Kristen and I to firmly agree on what was ahead in the immediate. She'd apply for an emergency family medical leave extension; she'd already been in touch with the school district. I'd rescind my two-week notice at the office jobs. Kristen's mother suggested we try to find a cheaper apartment out in Flushing, Queens, where there was an apartment building managed by her cousins. We loved where we were in Astoria but would need every dime we could save. Kristen wouldn't be paid for however long she was on leave. We'd now be a one-income family. Mine.

Later, I called Randy and told her I'd be at the next rehearsal. Already, I wanted to get on with everything, not only play rehearsal, but every one of my jobs. The week had obliterated any ideas about life after Kristen's maternity leave and any pleasure in thinking about it. I was glad to have the work. I'd look for even more.

"See you tomorrow then," Randy said, happy that I was happy.

Then, Michael called me. He'd been kept up to date by George.

"It's permanent," I told him. "But it's treatable. They've put her on meds. Everything else is normal. Fine."

"She'll be joining a roster of greats!" Michael said.

"Yeah?"

"Napoleon, Caesar, Byron, Tolstoy, Teddy Roosevelt," he said. "She'll be just another famous success who has epilepsy!"

I laughed.

"And there's Molière too! A playwright!" Michael added.

"That's right," I said. "That's absolutely right."

I looked over at George and told him what Michael had just said. George had tears in his eyes, nodding and smiling. It had been many years since we three had been roommates, but there and then, I needed my friends more than ever, like I needed to get back to rehearsal, needed to get back to all my jobs. I needed everything and everyone I had.

CHAPTER FIVE

HONEYMOON PERIOD

W e got to within a few months of Anna's second birthday without a seizure.

"Marc," said Donald Trump. "You're doing a great job."

"Thank you," I said.

"You married?"

"I am."

"Good," he said. "Kids?"

"One," I said.

He bumped his fists together and puckered his lips in approval, then shook my hand. He was standing on a "half apple" crate to make him appear taller than me.

"Boy or girl?" Trump asked.

"A girl. Anna."

"Great job," he said again.

"Thank you," I said. "It's been pretty messy."

"Always is," he said.

We were holding for the grip behind the camera to adjust a light. An assistant makeup artist swooped in to touch me up. Trump's personal makeup person swooped in to touch him up.

She, like his personal bodyguard, was always within a few feet of him since he arrived on set.

"Okay," called the second assistant director. "We're going again!"

"We're going again, Marc," Trump said.

"Let's do it, Donald," I said.

The quick scene we were doing involved only the two of us and took about forty minutes to shoot. We had to stand face to face, about a foot apart, in front of a Macy's display counter of Trump Accessories ties. Our director was Barry Levinson.

"Rolling!" called the camera person.

"Speed!" called the sound person.

The numbers were called, the sticks clapped, and we did our bit for the seventh or eighth time that morning.

It was March 2008, and this was not President Donald Trump, but *The Apprentice* and Trump Accessories pitchman Donald Trump. I'd done commercials with big names before, but this Macy's campaign, which had begun before the holidays a few months earlier, was loaded. I'd landed two national "spots" in the campaign. The first was with celebrity chef Emeril Lagassé. This one, aside from Trump, would have Mariah Carey, Martha Stewart, and Santana in it. And me.

I resisted trying to talk to Levinson. Trump seemed to like to chat, even making the rounds during the break to shake hands with the crew, while Levinson barely spoke to anyone but his assistant director. He even seemed to ignore Trump. I wanted to tell him that I'd seen *The Natural* about a thousand times as a kid, and how much it meant to just about every baseball player I knew. Nearly every morning of high school summers, my three brothers and I (they were all baseball players too) watched it on VHS. At some point, we had to ask my parents to buy us a second tape after wearing the first one out, especially at the end when Robert Redford hits the home run into the light tower. Now here I was working with the director. I was playing a customer being sold a Donald Trump tie by Trump himself. While Mariah and Santana jammed over her perfume line a few aisles away, Trump proclaimed to me, "My ties are so beautiful, they don't need music!" The scene lasted about three seconds in the final cut.

This was my first commercial shoot of 2008. I already had three other national network spots running while shooting this one and had reached an earnings level that insured our health coverage well into the following year and a half. I was auditioning multiple times a week, which was great, but it also further complicated my already near-impossible work schedule.

An actor gets a call less than twenty-four hours before commercial auditions, which are held at studios anywhere from Midtown to the Financial District. There is little negotiating room for whatever appointment time you get assigned, so most auditions throw the next day's plans into emergency rearrangement. And the odds of actually booking a commercial job are always extremely long. Casting could see many hundreds or even thousands of actors, sometimes in multiple cities, for any one role.

When I got one, though, it was more than worth the hassle. The money was great. I once did a Heineken spot that took six hours to shoot and paid about $80,000. Maybe equally as important as the money was that it could feel like everyone in my life, past and present, saw me on TV as what appeared to be a success. Aside from that, there was the thrill of this weird, temporary, anonymous fame. I would get odd looks from strangers on the subway—and occasionally one would even say, "Hey, aren't you the guy in..."

Of course, I loved when that happened. Any actor, especially a struggling one, would. And it happened a lot, probably because I was on the subway a lot. After all, I was still running back and forth between all my jobs. Strangers telling me they loved one of my commercials was always a welcome boost of encouragement, even if it set me back a few minutes on my train work, grading papers, or making lesson plans.

I was exhausted, but I usually didn't feel it. Things were going well. At City College, after my first year of teaching only one class per semester, I was assigned more writing workshops and lit courses. I'd never thought I'd qualify to teach literature at the college level, but the English Chair insisted I give it a go, and I loved it. In one class that involved realism and modernism, we studied Ibsen's *A Doll's House*, the play where the wife, Nora, walks out on her stubborn husband, and Kafka's *The Metamorphosis*, where the overworked Gregor wakes up one morning as a bug and eventually dies in his room. Both stories hit home.

Six months before the Macy's shoot with Trump, Kristen said we should have another child. I couldn't imagine it, risking another health disaster like we'd had with Anna, or worse. It would also mean Kristen would extend her work leave even longer, taking advantage of her legal right to maternity leave number two. I'd never have time to write another play again, I said. No way. Impossible.

Kristen countered with two arguments. First, she said it was now of utmost importance that Anna have a sibling, considering her medical condition. What if something happened to us? I didn't buy it, but the second angle worked. She kindly told me that if I didn't agree to have our second child, she'd have to leave me and find another means of providing Anna with a sibling.

After intense negotiations, or really what was mostly whining on my part, I agreed to all her terms. We'd have child number two, and Kristen would take another maternity leave, at the end of the emergency family medical leave to maximize her time off. I'd remain the sole earner for another two and a half years. The only privilege I won in all of this was that I got to decide this second child's name. In homage to my predicament, and love of literature, it would be Gregor if a boy and Nora if a girl.

Since Anna's PICU discharge over a year earlier, Kristen and I had some new routines. Constant vigilance was one. Anna had to be watched every hour of every day and night, so Kristen slept by her side in our bed. I took the sofa. Especially during the first few months, the anticipation of another seizure was constant. In our crash education on epilepsy, we learned that statistics showed that people with epilepsy face a far higher rate of suicide, mental health issues, learning and relationship problems, and of course, SUDEP. We would read another bad news article nearly every day. This hardly set the stage for much romance between us. But as the months since our discharge had proceeded without any seizures, by the time I was on set with The Donald, Kristen was four months pregnant, due that summer with…Nora.

Another new routine was making sure whoever was with Anna had on them the little black case. In it was a plastic syringe the size of a small handgun loaded with Anna's "rescue medicine." This was a liquid dose of Diazepam, a drug of a class called benzodiazepines. It was Valium, and theoretically powerful enough to shut seizures down. We were only supposed to use it in emergencies, meaning Anna was having another seizure cluster (more than three seizures in an hour) or a seizure lasting more than five minutes. In either of these cases, she was to get the Diazepam, delivered rectally.

Then, there was the blood testing. At first, Anna had them every couple of weeks to track her medicine levels and liver, which worked overtime processing the meds. As instructed, we had steadily decreased the Phenobarb and replaced it with the Oxcarbazepine. Anna had at first showed dangerously high liver functioning from the Phenobarb, but things were improving.

Anna hated the blood tests. We all did. They came at the end of each doctor appointment. The technician would tie a rubber tourniquet around Anna's bicep so the faint, blue vein would rise to the surface on the inside of her elbow. Then Anna would scream. She would scream for the entire process, the rubbing alcohol cleaning the skin, the tech finding the vein, the needle prick, the blood pumping into the vials, the needle removal, and even while the tech drew a smiley face on the Band-Aid. Her screaming was so intense and sustained that the blood test results always showed a low carbon dioxide reading.

After every doctor visit, where she'd get the blood test and have her med doses raised, she seemed unable or unwilling to laugh for days. Whether it was the trauma of the needle or her system adjusting to the med hike, we could never be sure—but we noticed that even when she came back around to her lively self, we never heard the beautiful sound of the belly laugh she once had.

Medicine time was another new routine. Twice each day, we had to deliver the two liquid meds by a smaller syringe into her mouth, battling her attempts to evade it. She'd cry when she detected it was coming, then close her little mouth, shake her head violently, kick, arch her back, punch, and roll until we pinned her down. We'd pry her mouth open and shoot the stuff down her throat. We had no choice. If we didn't get it down deep enough, she'd spit it out. In the early morning we had to wake her up for it, and twelve hours later, do it again. One time we left the Oxcarbazepine bottle too close, and she kicked it over, spilling it onto the floor. It was a weekend, and it took me most of the next day to track down the neurologist for an emergency refill prescription, then a pharmacist who was open on Sundays.

Because Anna fought so hard, it was too difficult for Kristen to administer the meds alone, one hand with the syringe, one hand on Anna. So I would do whatever I could to get home in time to assist. I hated giving these meds even more than I hated the blood tests. Kristen reported that Anna would kiss pictures of me when I wasn't home. When I was there, she'd crawl and cling to my ankle if I tried to leave the room for a moment. I was home so seldom that I couldn't help fearing that she would start associating her father with nothing much else but this medicine experience she hated. Since I'd be up before anyone in the morning, I'd be the one waking her for the meds before I left, and when I came home, it was a big hug and kiss hello, then loading the syringes.

Slowly, steadily, with each week that passed without a seizure, we began to invest our hopes in the idea that epilepsy could be something kept at bay and that her childhood could be normal. We knew other parents who had children with conditions like severe allergies, asthma, and diabetes. No doubt they felt much the same way we did at first learning about it, but their kids were each proceeding with life and thriving, one with a nebulizer, another avoiding eggs and nuts, and the other wearing a blood sugar monitor nobody even knew was hooked onto his waist. We felt that if we treated Anna as if there were nothing wrong with her, and expected all the things from her life that we were supposed to expect, then she would follow suit.

We had a great example to follow. Anna's cousin, a twin, was born with one of his arms underdeveloped—he appeared as if he had lost half an arm. Matthew, six or seven years old at this point, seemed to not even notice it, or care, and thrived in whatever he wanted to do. He even joked about his arm, telling enthralling tales about shark attacks, and rejected the prosthetic fitted for him. This was due to his inborn natural character, of course, but also the result of his parents' unwillingness to let him feel any less capable than anyone else. His father once quipped that the only thing he worried about was Matthew tying shoes. We intended to take their approach with Anna, hoping that Anna's issue, quite unlike Matthew's, since it was invisible, would be kept buried by a simple daily dose of a medicine.

Things were improving in other ways too. Ironically, I was gaining more and more opportunity in the areas I thought would suffer the most with Kristen staying out of work. Instead of falling behind, I felt I was actually gaining ground. Maybe it was the sheer relief of surviving the initial seizure cluster, but I was enjoying everything I was doing, even the office jobs. I'd begun to find the three or four hours I'd spend at the insurance agency doing busy work as a nice break, simple and mindless. My time at the periodontist typing job felt the same. Often, when the rest of the people in the office had already gone home, I'd be sitting all by myself in a small, comfortable converted closet, just me and the computer table. It was the only alone time I had in my life. I had long ago realized that having work, any work, was a great blessing. Having nonstop work felt like an even greater one. The commercials I had running were high profile: Verizon, ESPN, Toyota, and Macy's. Money and morale were on the rise.

We'd also moved to Flushing into a two-bedroom apartment. It was the Queens Koreatown, which ran right up against the Queens Chinatown. Further away from Manhattan, we'd pay much lower rent. The living room was spacious, and Anna made great use of it. She liked running around its hardwood floors, like she was doing wind sprints. We had her "library" set up in one of the corners, beneath a set of tall windows, where I'd read her Dr. Seuss books and the occasional Shakespeare. We'd sit on beanbags. Anna would pull a book from her plastic shelf and hand it to me. I'd make it about halfway through before she'd hand me another. I'd stop abruptly and look at her, as if shocked by the rude interruption. She'd laugh, then thrust the next one into my hand. We would proceed like this until the shelves were empty, and all the books, half-read, were scattered around us on the floor.

There would be an occasional Sunday when I might find myself being up to date on the periodontist letters, free of rehearsals, performances, classes, and auditions. I could stay home, and if the weather was good, we might take a walk to one of the small concrete city parks nearby and hit the swings, or I'd carry Anna on my back to explore the neighborhoods centered at the famously colorful, fragrant, and bustling Roosevelt Avenue and Main Street.

By the time Kristen announced the positive pregnancy test reading that heralded Nora's coming, much worry had been put aside. Everything that Kristen said in support of having another child made sense to me now. I was seeing for myself that my life was far richer with children in it. And the professional opportunities were still there. In fact, they seemed to have multiplied. While I hung on to the receptionist and typist gigs, some extraordinary things continued to happen for me as an actor and writer. I was flown to Los Angeles to film yet another commercial. The theatre department at Wake Forest hired me to come down for a three-day residency to give playwriting workshops. I continued to do plays at Axis. I was saying yes to every theatre opportunity, as I'd always done. In Anna's first twenty months, aside from the commercials, I acted in five plays, getting my name in a *New York Times* review of one of them, directed a one-act in the NYC Fringe Festival at the SoHo Playhouse, did some public play readings, and a two-line part opposite actor Christian Camargo in an independent film Randy directed.

The Phenobarb was completely weaned by spring and still, no seizures. Kristen and I felt like maybe we'd made it out of the woods. Kristen and Anna attended a happy slew of "Mommy and Me" classes. One was at a dance studio, another at a music school, another was at an indoor "farm," where they played with small animals, and yet another was an indoor, rubberized playground for toddlers. Once a week, there was the ballet studio, where the kids stood in a circle learning basic steps, while someone played nursery rhymes on the piano. Anna loved them all, and for Kristen, they served as a much-needed social outlet. She was out of the apartment and began to make new friends with other young moms. The classes were all in Manhattan, and they had Manhattan prices, but we were able to afford them thanks to the cheaper rent and my steady work.

One of the reasons we chose to do these things in Manhattan was so that I could occasionally stop in and participate. If I had some time between jobs, I'd swing by and take Kristen's place. I'd hold Anna straight as she struck a first position at ballet, clap along with a song at the music school, or roll a ball at the indoor playground.

Sometimes I couldn't help looking around with envious fascination at the other parents. I wondered what it was like for them to have never seen their children seize, have to wonder when they would again, or know the sounds and faces of fear, as we did at every blood test and medicine time. I fought these musings off as best I could, but it wasn't easy and may have prevented me from being as social as Kristen was at these places. I didn't make any friends.

The blood tests became less frequent as Anna's height and body weight naturally increased, even as we kept a steady increase of the Oxcarbazepine. Dr. Solomon continued to be very happy with how it seemed to be working. Not only was it considered one of the lightest anti-seizure drugs on the market, in terms of side effects, but it seemed to be successful even when Anna caught a cold or a bit of winter cruds. When sufferers of epilepsy get sick, their "threshold" is often lowered, and "breakthrough" seizures can happen. So far, nothing had broken through. Ideally, Anna would stay on this medicine indefinitely, at a low dose, feel no negative effects, and never have a seizure again. We were told that about 75 percent of people with epilepsy find their condition able to be controlled by medication. All signs were that Anna would be on the fortunate side of this statistic.

One Sunday a couple weeks after the Macy's shoot, walking to rehearsal at Axis, I noticed a small sign on a graffitied stage door on 8th Street. A small Off-Off-Broadway theatre group I'd never heard of was producing one of my older plays called *Carl the Second*. I immediately called George, who had directed the premiere years before, and we agreed we had to go see it that weekend. Since we'd first produced this play years before, some colleges and community theatres had done it in different cities, but they were too far away for me to attend. This was a unique opportunity.

We brought along some other close friends, like David Elliott, who had originally produced the show. David was yet another old friend who went on to the big time, winning a Tony Award for a play he produced at Lincoln Center.

We sat in the back row of the small black box theatre. *Carl* is a dark comedy about a young man with a huge inferiority complex. After a lifetime of only near-triumphs and near-successes, he becomes convinced he's meant to be "second" in everything he tries to do, never a "first." He comes to embrace this role in life and even prefer it. He finds it safer to expect and even revel in near misses with success rather than success itself. The problem comes when he meets the love of his life and lets his life approach do everything it can to ruin his chance at happiness.

My play looked and sounded different with this group than it had when our company did it, but they made it work. It gave us so many happy memories of our own six-week run on 29th Street. *Carl* was my first full-length play and the first reviewed in any major press. *The Village Voice* wrote a funny little capsule blurb, but *Time Out* did a full review with a photo, which included some very generous comments about the play, George's direction, and the cast. Nowadays, reviews usually post online before any print versions, but back when *Carl* opened, it was different. After an opening night, theatre people would wait in the early morning at newsstands known for getting the city's first stacks. We'd buy the magazine or paper and breathlessly flip the pages until we found our show's review. I remembered that morning on Astor Place, seeing the new *Time Out* dropped off in its bundles, buying one, finding the page, frantically reading, and exhaling in joy that the compliments outweighed the quibbles. It was one of many "New York Writer" moments I've been so lucky to have. "New York Writer" moments aren't always happy, but that one was. As I watched this same play all these years later on 8th Street, laughing and remembering, I reflected on how grateful I should feel, having found a place, however small, in the theatre world.

We'd chosen the matinee to attend that day so that I could be home in Flushing for medicine time, and I got there about twenty minutes late. The doctors had told us not to worry about slight variations in dose time—twenty minutes would hardly matter— but still, we tried to keep it regular. I had called Kristen a few times on the elevated 7 train to update her on my ETA, and she repeatedly told me not to stress.

I opened our door, walked in, hung my jacket on the hook and headed straight for the medicine cabinet. I was walking fast, right past Anna and Kristen in the living room.

"Dadda!" Anna called.

"Hello!" I said, already in the bathroom, at the medicine cabinet.

"We did the meds!" Kristen called. "She did great. Right Anna?"

"Yah!" she said, with a squeal.

"Right on time. She didn't even complain."

"What?" I said. "Can it be?"

I came back to the living room.

"I told her you were on your way home and you were worried about it," Kristen said. "And she took them no problem."

Anna was beaming, decked out in full ballet dress: leotard, tights, a tutu; even the shoes. She was standing in front of the sofa on the coffee table surface, which had been cleared off like a stage.

"Be careful!" I said. I hadn't yet noticed Kristen had put the beanbags, pillows and cushions all around.

"We've been rehearsing," Kristen said. "You're in for a show."

"Dance show!" Anna said, bursting with excitement.

"She's so excited to dance for us," Kristen said as I sat next to her on the sofa. She turned back to Anna. "Are you ready to do your show?"

"Ready!"

Anna took a bow, and I applauded.

"Is there more?" I said, laughing.

"Ready Anna?" Kristen said. Anna gave one, firm nod that almost threw her forward. "Go!"

Anna took first position. I applauded again. Kristen pressed a button on the stereo remote and classical music began to play. Anna straightened her torso. She looked like a dancer. A real dancer.

"Second position!" Kristen called out. Anna shifted. Then third, then fourth, then fifth.

"Plié!" Kristen called out. Anna brought her arms in front of her, then slowly bent her legs at the knees.

We clapped. She went through more. Relevé, passé…

"Arabesque!" Kristen said. Anna struck the position, one leg flat to the table surface, the other out behind her. I couldn't believe it. She was balancing. I applauded again.

Anna kept glancing at me throughout, and I made sure to be looking right in her eyes when she did, with a dazzled expression. This time on her own, without any direction from Kristen, she retook fifth position, put her hands on her waist, and attempted a pirouette. She spun almost halfway around before losing her balance, heading for the table edge. As she stumbled, an expression of confusion came across her face. Something was wrong, and she looked at me as if she knew I could, and would, stop it.

I jumped forward off the sofa and snatched her before what would have probably been a fun drop onto the puffy pillow. Still, my heart felt like it would shoot through my sternum. Anna started laughing, then Kristen was laughing, and eventually so was I, but there was something in me lingering. I was full of something, a chemical, a sound, a kind of maximum sensation. It took a few minutes to wear off, and until it did, I held Anna against me, telling her I loved her and that she was a dancer, a real and very beautiful dancer.

Kristen began to return the beanbags to the library corner and the cushions onto the sofa, and I brought the pillows back into our bedroom. We started talking about dinner.

I stood beside Kristen in our tight galley kitchen and we cooked and talked, mostly about how great Anna was doing at dance and how the classes were clearly worth the money. As food began to heat, Anna came walking in and held my leg.

"Hi Anna," I said. "Smell the food?"

"Hi," she said again. "Dadda."

I wasn't looking down at her. I was looking at whatever I was doing on the counter. I could feel her slip off my leg and sit beside me. I realized then that we'd left the music playing in the living room. *The Nutcracker.*

"Anna, not a good place to sit," I said. I could feel a hand back on my leg, as if reaching for it to pull herself up. I still hadn't looked down.

"Maybe we should take off your ballet stuff? Put pajamas on?" Kristen said, washing a pot. "We're going to eat, and you don't want stains on your ballet clothes!"

Anna didn't answer. I felt her move across my foot. I looked down and she was on her belly. Her right leg and arm were making circular movements, as if riding a bicycle. She made a muffled groan. I grabbed her, held her up, and looked into her eyes.

"Seizure," I said to Kristen.

We'd come to the end of the honeymoon. The doctors steadily increased the Oxcarbazepine, as the seizures became more frequent. At first, they broke through once or twice monthly, then it was weekly. The dosage was approaching the limit, based on what the doctor could glean from the blood tests. They added a second medicine, Levetiracetam. It didn't have an effect. Anna was getting worse. By midsummer, she was seizing at least twice a day.

On August 6, 2008, exactly two years, two months, and two days after we had our first child, Nora was born at Lenox Hill Hospital in Manhattan. A week later, Anna was admitted to the NYU Langone Medical Center. After Dr. Solomon at NewYork-Presbyterian had announced her retirement, a family friend recommended a pediatric epileptologist there. This doctor ordered Anna weaned off all medicine, then slowly introduced a stronger drug called Divalproex Sodium, all under close inpatient supervision.

When we checked Anna in, it seemed she remembered her first experience in a PICU. The difference now was that she had words and sentences. She could be heard across the unit. Maybe the hospital. Maybe the city.

"Take me home!" she screamed. "Please!"

They held her down on the bed, glued the EEG leads down, took the blood from her arm, and stuck the IV into the top of her hand.

"I miss my baby sister!" she was crying now, over and over. She had met Nora for a mere matter of hours. "I miss Nora! No more doctors!"

She saw me, standing at a distance behind the nurses and techs, watching.

"Please, Daddy. Help me!"

I looked away.

"Help me, Daddy."

Louder and louder, again and again, until it dried out her throat, and brought it nearly to a breathless whisper.

"Help me."

Our parents split the cost of a nearby hotel room so that Kristen could run from the hospital, feed Nora, then return to be with Anna. It would be twelve days in NYU's PICU before the new medicine began to work. Among the side effects we were told to expect were hair loss, vision difficulty, weight gain, and muscle weakness.

She started nursery school a month later.

CHAPTER SIX

POT, POISON, AND AN ABNORMAL NORMAL

A fter I stared awhile through my window at the Mercy softball field, trying to believe Anna went peacefully back to class, I sat back down at my computer. Scrolling over the links to the marijuana articles, I thought about how many medicines had failed over the years. We had long since accepted that Anna's case was not among those able to be fully controlled on medication, but still clung hard to the possibility that the delayed myelination would complete itself, and clung just as hard to the luck that Anna's seizures didn't attack her while she was awake. But now it felt like this was the end of yet another honeymoon period. After having settled into a kind of abnormal normal for years, a fresh set of horrendous possibilities had arrived.

I skimmed a few more reports on marijuana overdose, then finally picked up the phone and called Dr. Chin. She said she was in a meeting but would be free within the hour. Despite how busy and sought after she was, it never took her long to get back to me. She had practices in California, New York City, and Westchester. She was on the cover of magazines, did major television interviews, and had been a leader in the research and application of medical cannabis for decades.

As I waited, I got more and more anxious to speak with her, hoping she'd have the perfect explanation for these past few days, and the perfect solution. I tried to turn my focus back to my Understanding Movies class, where I'd be screening Lamorisse's *The Red Balloon* in about ninety minutes.

I went over some notes for my lecture but quickly found myself right back on the internet, scouring reports on cases of children having bad reactions to marijuana and what a recovery from it might be like. If what we'd experienced with Anna over the last few days was in fact such a reaction, would there be permanent damage? Could it all repair itself upon withdrawal? Or over time? And how much time?

The first we heard about the connection between marijuana and the treatment of epilepsy was the same way many others first heard of it. CNN broadcast a special with Dr. Sanjay Gupta in 2013, when Anna was seven, taking a drug called Lamotrigine, the sixth medication she'd been on. Dr. Gupta had been researching the health benefits of marijuana for some time and had now officially "changed course" in his thinking on it, which meant he was now in favor of it. He even apologized to the world for not initially supporting it.

At the time of his reporting, the test subjects for medical cannabis were among the most severely stricken with seizure disorders, like Dravet Syndrome. They were children with scores of unstoppable daily seizures. These patients were all emergency cases, far worse even than Anna's, and made the best subjects for gathering fast data, since the CBD oil would either cause immediate lessening of seizures, or it wouldn't. It proved a success for many of these patients, who had had little or none with pharmaceuticals. Cannabis was saving lives.

This news spread across the epilepsy community, bringing huge hope. Not only was this stuff stopping seizures, it was a natural plant extract, not a molecular invention with the debilitating side effects so many people on anticonvulsants had come to know. Additionally, this treatment could be used on kids because CBD was the element of marijuana that didn't cause the high. There was only a tiny amount of the psychoactive THC in the oil.

Not everyone was on board, doctors included. Even at this point, after some states outside New York legalized its use, people had expressed their trepidation about trying cannabis on Anna. My Aunt Maureen didn't feel comfortable when I first told her. She felt there was a lack of sufficient data for or against it and had heard stories of children hospitalized with nasty reactions. Any time we brought it up with our neurologist, despite NYU being the home of much of the highest-profile cannabis research, we never seemed to get much of an interested response.

Still, to many, cannabis was the medical miracle of our age. Before it was legalized more widely, desperate parents with suffering children were uprooting their entire lives, moving to states where medical marijuana was legal. Gupta used some of these stories in his special.

Capitalizing on all the big press, the industry of CBD products drawn from the hemp plant became highly visible, and it was legal everywhere. The stuff epilepsy patients really wanted, we would come to understand, was the extract of the marijuana plant, which was the famous "Charlotte's Web" oil in Gupta's report. Many companies with very pleasant, outdoorsy-sounding brand names emerged selling hemp plant oil. This could certainly feel marketed at those like us, who may either be unaware that it was not the marijuana CBD, didn't know there was any difference, or were desperate enough to try it anyway. The makeup of the marijuana-derived CBD oil is different than that of the hemp plant and contains a necessary level of marijuana THC. In short, they look, smell, and sound like the same thing, but they aren't. Nonetheless, before New York legalized medical marijuana, we bought lots of the hemp product. While there may be health benefits to it, we never saw any effect on Anna's seizures.

Right around the time the CNN show aired, we'd moved to our house in Bayside, Queens, just east of Flushing. Both girls attended the public elementary school up the street. Anna's seizures were coming, all nocturnal, and irregularly. There were good weeks, and there were bad weeks. Steadily, with Anna's waking life now passing as relatively normal, and with Lamotrigine not having many side effects, a kind of complacency set in, a grim acceptance that until that hoped-for moment the myelination did its thing in her brain, Anna's life would be exhausting, often frightening, but livable.

These were the years of that abnormal normal. Kristen and I slept in different rooms, so one of us could be with Anna. While she was small, she'd sleep beside Kristen in the queen-sized bed in our room, while I took the sofa. As she grew larger, she would be in her own small bed in her room, with me on the floor. At dawn, Kristen and I would pass each other in the hall. Before anything else was spoken, whoever was with Anna the night before would hold up however many fingers for however many seizures she had. A thumbs up meant she had a peaceful night. Then, we'd decide who would shower first, discuss the business of the day, mood determined by that number of fingers.

Nonetheless, both girls were growing up happy and thriving at school, taking their dance classes, and Kristen and I hustled to and from our jobs around their schedules. As for Anna's prospects with alternative treatments, the most aggressive effort was maintained by Kristen's mother, a big believer in holistic medicine. Even as we, the parents, came to accept Anna's condition as a fixed part of our lives, at least for her childhood, Geri never gave up pursuing any and every route to healing she could find.

She researched tirelessly and over the years had us trying diets, supplements, chiropractors, acupuncturists, even CDs of soothing New Age music that claimed to have embedded "alpha waves" that would regulate brainwaves while you slept. None of it worked, but she never stopped looking for the next lead, new study, doctor, or therapy. Geri was a major proponent of trying CBD. Both kinds.

For these years, things generally stayed consistent. We saw little sign that anything was improving, but nothing worsened, either. The NYU doctor had said a solid majority of myelination cases resolve—and that Anna, having no other neurological issues, would hopefully fall in that majority. This was the statistic we tried to dwell on, but there were others that were hard to ignore. The fact that her seizures never became fully controlled by any med made it less likely we would ever see her outgrow them. This was depressingly stark, but I tried my best to believe that we would not always be living this fearful life. One day, it would be over. Gone. After all, it wasn't a lesion like they first thought. It was delayed myelination, a temporary problem. We were waiting it out, stalling, taking a knee; running out the clock until the happy ending.

We had every chip our minds and souls had left to wager on the idea that what Anna had was a "childhood epilepsy." We didn't discuss it often, probably because we'd have to acknowledge to each other that, of course, it could last her entire life, that for so many people with this insidious condition, it does just that. Better to focus on enduring the nights, trying med after med after med, and getting through the day without going mad.

*

We'd had to find a nursery school for Anna with a full-time nurse who was trained and licensed to deliver the rescue med if it came to it. Most preschools for two-year-olds didn't have a nurse, so we had no choice but to pay over $12,000 out of our quickly-sinking savings for a program that was part of a private school. Anna was doing fine at first on the Divalproex Sodium. In fact, after a few months in the nursery school, the teachers suggested she be moved up to the three-year-old class, since she seemed "advanced" and more attentive, articulate, and compliant than the other two-year-olds in the group.

We didn't get to celebrate this report for very long. It turned out we'd been on another honeymoon, and it would be shorter than the first. By Christmas of her second year in pre-school, the Divalproex began to fail just as the Oxcarbazepine had. The seizures were breaking through day and night despite her being on a high dosage, and so, once again, Anna was hospitalized and put on an additional medication. This one was called Zonisamide. Whether it was the drug itself, or the combination, we'll never know, but Anna would have an extreme adverse reaction. Within a few weeks of mixing those two meds, Anna lost a year of cognitive development, the ability to walk straight and even hold a crayon in her fingers.

They rushed a withdrawal in four days, but the damage was done. From that point, Anna would have rehabilitative services, physical and cognitive, throughout her childhood and a special education classification. The way she formed sentences, processed language, and recalled from short-term memory had been affected for the worse. Beyond our pain over these wounds was the crushing knowledge that we had been giving our child something that was hurting her body, nerves, and brain.

Anna was nine by the time New York Governor Andrew Cuomo signed a bill approving medical marijuana into law. This was good news, but it would take some time to actually get it, and any time felt like too much time. The entire program had to be set up with specially-licensed doctors, dispensaries, and a patient registration system. Until all that was figured out, what was available to people in New York was only the hemp CBD, unless you became a drug smuggler. So I became one.

One afternoon between my classes, I was having coffee at a cramped little café near the City College campus, commiserating with my friend Nicole Treska, a fellow writer and English department adjunct. This was 2014. There were major budget cuts rumored to be ahead, and we were convinced we'd be losing our already-underpaid teaching jobs. Cuomo and Bill de Blasio, the New York Mayor, had begun to use the CUNY budget as a political football. The governor claimed CUNY was self-sustaining and that only the city should subsidize it. The mayor said the state can't pull its funding without destroying the system. Word spread through the humanities division that if cuts happened, many of our programs and classes would be eliminated. There was always a general instability as it pertained to job security for us, but at this juncture, it seemed the great budget apocalypse that would end all adjunct life was finally going to happen.

This was a dark prospect. For years, senior members of my department had spoken with great sincerity about my becoming full time someday. Now, I felt I'd be lucky to keep what I already had. I'd recently read an article explaining how it was currently the worst time in the history of American higher education for new hires in the arts and humanities. These jobs were already hard to get; now, they were essentially impossible.

Kristen had been back to work for a few years by now, and I had finally left my other office jobs, but now, I felt I was descending to a professional low. I was forty-four, had two kids (one with a chronic health condition), a thirty-year mortgage, credit card debt, and was barely piecing together a working-class income teaching two or three courses a semester and working Off-Off-Broadway theatre jobs that paid about $350 a week. I hadn't done a commercial in three years. My agent told me I had fallen into a strange zone casting-wise: too young looking to play the dad, too old to play the young man. My "look" was out too. I could see that. Suddenly, all the guys in commercials had thick beards, the kind that would take me five years to grow. It seemed to me that a more lively, diverse, "hipster look" was in, not the "white, tired, spaced-out, worried former jock," which was how I liked to describe my own "look." Kristen made more money than I did, thank goodness, but it wasn't enough to keep us afloat, not even close. If I lost my classes, it would mean a $25,000 hit.

Nicole and I talked about what we'd do if this budget thing happened. She said she'd look for freelance editing work, rent her bedroom through Airbnb, and sleep in a closet. I figured I'd first start with the most unlikely solution: looking for teaching jobs elsewhere at other colleges and maybe even high schools. I thought I'd get back into coaching baseball, though I hadn't stepped on a diamond in a long while and really had no idea how I'd go about returning. I started thinking how ridiculous it was that at my age, I had so few things I could do for money. And as if our conversation wasn't enough of a bummer, Nicole then asked me about Anna.

She didn't personally know Anna, or Nora, or Kristen, outside of some photos and comments on Facebook. I posted a lot about my kids on Facebook. Nora was a gifted illustrator, and nearly every time she produced a portrait, or in some cases an entire storyboard of beautifully expressive characters and dialogue, I'd post it with pride. If either of the girls were dancing on the sidewalk or in the house, acting in a school play, or just standing around looking happy, I'd snap and post. If I was in a play, or one I'd written was being done somewhere, I'd use Facebook to spread the word. For me, Facebook was a place for sharing shiny good news and promoting my work, but every now and then, I'd write about Anna's epilepsy. I'd post a picture of her in a hospital bed waving to the camera or congratulate her on playing a full soccer game after a night of seizures. I figured she may someday resent me for publicizing her medical condition, but my thinking was that the more people who knew, the more of a chance that someone with experience with epilepsy, firsthand or otherwise, might offer a lead to something helpful.

I joined epilepsy support groups on Facebook like "Epilepsy Awareness," "My Epilepsy Team," "All about life with Epilepsy," and others. These groups can have tens of thousands of members, and the posts are often written by the sufferers themselves, looking for information on meds, about what to expect from this or that test, or just reaching out for support. Sometimes, I'd see posts written by a loved one, sharing the news of a death. These were all often agonized posts, but could seem to bring some consolation to the writer. There are fifty million people in the world with epilepsy, and it can seem like each patient's personal version of the disorder is unique. Any fellowship could be an enormous comfort.

"Anna's been the same," I said to Nicole. "By day, she sort of lives a normal nine-year-old's life. At night, we live with the seizures. The awful moments come, then we go back to sleep. It's hell, but it's not that bad, I guess, judging by what I've seen in those hospitals."

"How does Nora handle it?" she said. I was touched by this question. Even I so often don't consider Nora's experience with all this, and here was someone who doesn't even know her, asking about it.

"It's something we don't think about enough, I'm sure. It kills me to know that she's exposed to all this fear in her family."

"It must be hard for her."

"The other night, Nora asked if she could try something. She asked if she could sleep next to Anna. We said sure, and as I got myself ready on the floor, I saw that Nora had placed her hand on Anna's head. She slept like that all night, like that would protect her sister. It killed me."

"I love her art," Nicole said. "The kid is talented."

"Yes," I said. "I just hope her skin is thick."

"Have you tried the CBD?" Nicole said. It was a question lots of people had asked me.

"Well, we can only get the hemp stuff right now. We tried it. Did nothing. There's no way to get the real stuff yet."

"I can get the real stuff."

"What?"

"I'm from Colorado. My friend works at a distributor in Denver."

"Tell me what to do," I said.

Over the following weeks, Nicole made contact with her Denver friend, and I put cash aside. It wasn't medical marijuana, but rather marijuana-derived CBD "recreational" chocolate chews. They were nearly $200 for a box of twenty-five. Her friend was all for getting it to us, and said he'd order the chews for the store, putting as much in stock as possible without his bosses becoming suspicious. These low-THC chews weren't exactly huge sellers. Nicole happened to be planning a visit soon and said that if the stuff had been shipped to the store by the time she got there, I could put the money in her bank account here in New York. She'd buy the chews in Colorado, then fly back with them.

"On a plane? What if you get caught?"

"Do it all the time. You stick it in the checked baggage."

I was already afraid, just talking about doing this. When she called from Denver and said the chews had come in and that she could get me a few boxes, to go ahead and put the money into her account, I was sure I'd be arrested as soon as I entered the bank lobby. I had similar visions for what would happen when I actually obtained the contraband, or once I was actually putting it into my child's mouth, which I assumed was technically child abuse.

I'd smoked pot three times in my life, and all three times, it had no effect on me except a mild dizziness and burning in the back of my throat. I took Advil for headaches and for my sore shoulder when I was still a pitcher. That was about it for my career with taking drugs. As for *buying* drugs, I had only the worst expectations. Still, if there was any chance it could help Anna, illegal interstate drug commerce felt worth a shot.

I kept quiet about our scheme for the most part. I told Kristen, Geri, my own parents, and, since we were a tight bunch, everyone at Axis. I knew the money issue would have to be dealt with at some point. Obviously, insurance didn't cover weed abstracts, and we had no idea how long one box would last, since we had no idea what dosage would work for Anna.

There was a branch of Nicole's bank in Bayside, but they wouldn't accept my cash as a deposit into someone else's account, so she put up the few hundred for me in Denver and flew back with the goods. I met her on campus a few days later to make the exchange. We sat at a small, wrought-iron table where, over the years, I'd read Homer, Sophocles, Shakespeare, Voltaire...name it...and made lecture notes. Now I was here buying a Schedule I narcotic, literally under the table.

What alternative was there? Once Nicole proposed it, not trying it might have driven me more crazy than I already was. Of course, now that I had access to these chews, I didn't want to get my hopes up, so I tried to keep the same thinking we'd have with any other new med. But it was hard not to dream. The medical reports on this substance were so powerful. I couldn't help thinking that at last, just like this, we'd figured out the right way to help our daughter.

I slipped Nicole the cash as she handed me a small cardboard box sealed with blue painter's tape and one strip of duct tape. The thing couldn't have looked more shady. We were laughing as we were doing this. I told her I was sure campus security had staked us out and that the college president was probably watching with binoculars from a window in Shepard Hall.

"Good luck, Marc," she said. "I hope it works."

I thanked her. I felt I might cry if I sat there any longer. We got up, and I headed to the subway, looking around, expecting a SWAT team to swarm in.

I rode the subway to Penn Station with the ridiculous-looking box in my backpack. I felt like I was carrying a bomb. The announcement about police having the right to examine bags at random came over the speaker twice between 125th and 34th Streets. I then had to walk past K-9 cops. My brother-in-law

Rich was one of those for the Metropolitan Transit Authority. He'd be assigned many different places each week, and every now and then, I'd see him with his German Shepherd, Jake. I'd stop, we'd chat, have some laughs, and I'd feel super cool. Now, I was praying Rich was assigned anywhere but Penn Station tonight, since Jake would likely sniff the dope and tackle me, even if he had enjoyed two Thanksgivings at my parents' house. The job comes first.

I made it home without incident. That night, we opened one of the boxes and unwrapped a chew. It looked like a little Milky Way bar, but it smelled like weed. Nicole's friend recommended we start by giving Anna a thin slice about an hour before she went to sleep, then build up until it was having its desired effect. I told Anna it was a new "health cracker." I put the other boxes into the fridge, then noticed a small baggie filled with other kinds of loose chews. There was a Post-it inside, reading, "For the parents. They need it."

He'd thrown in some high-THC products. Now I was sure I'd end up in jail. Even though I was alone in my own kitchen, my first instinct was to hide the stuff under my shirt and look around to make sure the coast was clear. I thought about throwing it right into the garbage, but I felt guilty about rejecting this stranger's kind gesture, so I stuck the baggie into the back of the fridge behind the salad dressings. I went upstairs and slept on Anna's floor, hopeful I wouldn't see a seizure that night and more than a bit amused that we had a considerably large stash of dope in the house.

We started a new, detailed calendar to keep track of the effect of the CBD. Each week, we doubled the sliver of chew. At first, we saw no difference in Anna's patterns, or lack of patterns. She'd have a night or two without a seizure, then a night with three or four, then back to none, or one, or two the next. The usual. When we got to half a chew, though, things changed. The stretches of peaceful nights started going beyond only a night or two, and Anna slept heavier. She shifted and changed positions less frequently, some nights not moving at all. This didn't allow me much better rest on the floor, since I was as afraid of not hearing something, even when there was nothing to hear.

The chews seemed to be doing something. Not only were there longer stretches of nights without activity; there were fewer seizures on the nights they did come. As we proceeded into that winter, Anna rarely had a night of more than two seizures and could reach as much as a week without any. We got all the way up to a full chew a night, which was 50mg of CBD, and were seeing her best nights in years.

At this rate, one box wouldn't even cover a month. But as we got the word out that this marijuana experiment was possibly working, people emerged with huge generosity. Geri and Kristen's father Bruce bought boxes, my own parents bought boxes, and one day at the theatre, Randy handed over ten, telling me that when those ran out, she'd buy more. This was all both extremely touching and a little sickening to me. I was ashamed at not being able to buy a limitless supply myself. I tried to take some comfort in the idea that New York State would eventually get its act together with the dispensaries, and doctors would prescribe it at lower prices and that insurance would be forced to pay.

One day after rehearsal, Randy handed me another box, and I tried to decline.

"What's the matter with you?" Randy said. "There's no shame in letting people help."

"I should have the money to take care of my own child," I said.

"It's Anna. And it's our honor to help her. That's what people are doing, not thinking about how much money Marc has. How about focusing on the fact that it's working!"

Nicole and I didn't lose our adjunct jobs. The fear of the budget cuts we discussed that day at the café proved unfounded. I got my course assignments for the next two semesters, both for my higher-paid MFA workshops and my undergrad classes. Axis hired me for its next three projects. I was seeing more commercial auditions again and even got one for *Boardwalk Empire* on HBO. My latest play that had run at Axis, *The Groundling*, got a decent notice in the *Times* and was starting to get produced in small professional theatres in other cities almost immediately after its publication.

I had no doubt that the effectiveness the CBD appeared to be showing had as much to do with how good I was feeling, as did the fact that CUNY didn't fold. I was professionally engaged again, after a dry spell, and it was as if a new engine was inside me. I wanted new starts. I had sent my resume to other colleges, particularly their theatre and English departments. One was for a job posting for a Speech and Performance assistant professor at Mercy College.

I also made my way back into baseball. I called an old friend and fellow high school coach. I learned Shaun Manning was no longer coaching at Chaminade High School, where we had met, but now ran an all-year travel baseball program called Next Level Baseball. Although I was only looking for his advice on how to start getting work doing private pitching lessons on the side, he asked me to join his organization. He invited me to their winter workout program one night for me to observe, then slapped a hundred-dollar bill in my hand just for coming. He asked me if I liked what he was doing with the players, and I told him I thought it was incredible, which it was. He asked me to be one of the program's pitching coaches. I officially had another job, back on the field, this time with a summer team, being paid twice what I'd been paid at the high school. Within a few months, I had a dozen private lesson clients as well.

This return to baseball felt like a homecoming. It was years since I'd last coached, and somehow, I'd forgotten how much my history as a player could impress people, and how lucky I was to have it. The Long Island and Queens amateur baseball world was a scene of people who knew me and my brothers, all of whom played Division I college ball and/or the minor leagues. People respected what we'd achieved, and it was a world where I had something of real value to contribute. The return also gave me a creative revival. I'd been tearing my hair out, trying to come up with an idea for my next play. I still didn't have much of a concept, but now, I thought it could be about a middle-aged man returning to the game he forgot he loved. It was a mood-lifter just to have a basic premise. As a playwright, I was always more productive when an idea evolved in my head awhile before I started putting it to paper, as opposed to the writers who dive into the blank page to see what happens.

Nora was loving school. She loved her teachers, had lots of friends, and her grades were high. Unlike Anna, Nora preferred to do all her work by herself. She'd come home, finish homework, and if she didn't have dance class, she'd draw. Faces and scenes and pages of stories with drawings she called her graphic novels. She even wrote some plays, with titles like "Get to Tomorrow," about a family gone camping only to be lost in the woods, and even a coming-of-age musical with a showstopping song called "I Know I'm Bad but I Want to Be Good."

By the time Anna was at her halfway point as a fifth grade "senior" at her elementary school, she'd moved up three reading levels and was elected Vice President of Student Council. She played CYO volleyball and softball, balancing all this with her dance classes and schoolwork. She was doing so well seizure-wise that Kristen and I asked the neurologist if we could start decreasing the Lamotrigine dose. It never fully worked anyway, and I now wondered if this med had actually been causing more seizures than it was suppressing. "Difficulty sleeping" was one of the possible side effects of Lamictal, and I formed a logic in my head that if she was only lightly asleep in the first place, couldn't this be giving the nocturnal seizures she was still occasionally having a better chance at breaking through? The doctor wasn't too keen on it, but by winter break that year, Anna was on half the Lamotrigine she'd been on at the start of the school year, and things had only gotten better. We had no idea why, of course. Maybe it was the CBD, maybe it was that myelination finally at the finish line.

It was a school night in mid-December when I remembered the little baggie our "source" had thrown into that first package from Denver. My fall semester had just ended. I'd read all the final papers and gotten my grades in. The Axis annual holiday show was open and running on the weekends. Homework for the girls was done for the evening, and Kristen was out at a holiday event at her school. It was just me and the kids, and I thought I'd make my special: French toast for dinner, one of the few dishes I was capable of. They loved the idea. We battered up the eggs together, then I lit the stovetop. I dipped the bread slices and threw them on the frying pan. I felt like a beer and looked in the fridge. No beer. I didn't feel like running to the deli to buy some, so I figured what the heck, I'd try one of those chews "For the parents."

Maybe I'd like it, I thought. Maybe that guy in Colorado knew what was best for me. The light stuff was helping my daughter, so why not give the heavy duty chews in the back of the fridge a go for myself? Maybe this will be healthy, I thought. Maybe all the drug tests in college the NCAA mandated left me with an irrational fear of drugs. I unwrapped one. The first thing I noticed was that it was a slightly different color than the ones Anna was taking. I popped the thing in my mouth, chewed, and swallowed.

For twenty minutes, as I fried the egg and milk-drenched slices of bread and served dinner, I felt only a slight tug at the top of my head, nothing unpleasant, just some tightness. Anna and Nora ate on fold-up trays in the living room in front of the television. We had made a deal that if they finished their homework without complaining, which they did, they could watch a movie while they ate.

I was washing the frying pan when it hit me. The slight tug turned into a whirling vertigo, pulling everything inside me to one direction. I started following the direction I was being pulled in, until I realized I was walking in small circles. I noticed then that the water was still running in the sink, and some pieces of bread had clogged the drain, causing the water to run over the side and onto my feet. I turned the faucet off, and when I brought my eyes toward the floor to see how much of a puddle I'd made, I felt like I was sliding down a steep slope. My stomach reeled, I felt like I would vomit, I hoped I would vomit, and started hobbling, step by heavy step, toward the stairs.

I intended on making it to our upstairs bathroom, which required me passing behind the girls as they faced the television. Each step was like I was underwater. My feet and legs felt enormous, and by now I was not only extremely nauseous and dizzy, but my head was throbbing. I let out a loud, aching sigh.

"Oh my God!" I said, getting to the stairs, placing one hand on the banister.

"What?" Nora said.

"Nothing! Just...tired!" I got out, or something like it.

I felt I was beyond vomiting and might just faint. Step by leaden step, I heaved myself up the stairs, pulling mightily on the banister.

Somehow, I got to the bathroom mirror, and it took whatever strength I could muster just to hold my head up long enough to look at myself. I was green. I had heard that you can be green, so sick that you actually turn green, but I'd never seen it. My skin had changed color completely, like a lizard. Everything hurt. I slowly turned the water on, moved my hands under it, and splashed it on my face. I again bellowed out some kind of pained noise. This time, the girls came running.

"Daddy!" Anna said. "What's wrong?"

"Daddy?" Nora followed. They didn't sound like it was an emergency, but like they were intrigued. I tried to respond, but my upper half felt so heavy that I couldn't get enough air into my lungs to form words. I just sighed.

"Are you sick?" Nora said.

"What's the matter?" Anna said.

The girls repeated their questions, which made my head hurt worse.

"Are you sick, Dad?"

"What's the matter?"

"Are you sick?"

"What's the matter?"

"Dad?"

"What's the matter?"

Finally, I grabbed the sides of the sink for support, took a deep, hard breath, and shouted:

"YOUR FATHER IS HIGH ON DRUGS! I'M DYING!"

I turned the faucet further for colder water. The girls stared. Anna asked if she should call Kristen. I shook my head no, the slight force of which nearly tossed me into the bathtub. Anna shrugged, turned, and headed back downstairs, leaving Nora in the threshold.

"You shouldn't do drugs," she said. "This is what happens."

"Yup," I muttered.

"And drugs are illegal, Dad."

Nora then turned and trotted down the stairs. Soon I heard the movie, which had been paused, resume.

I stood there at the sink, hoping desperately that nobody would show up at the house and see me like this or that I wouldn't just drop dead. At some point, it started to abate, and I made my way to my bed. Maybe an hour later, I woke up, feeling as if I had most of my faculties back. The television was still going downstairs. I looked at the clock on the dresser. It was after ten.

"Girls?" I called, twice, my voice raspy.

They both answered with a monotone, "What?"

I sat up. I was still off, but the worst of it was over. I slid off the bed and made it back downstairs, moving slow, but pretending like nothing ever happened. They were now into a second movie.

"Girls, brush teeth. It's late. Anna, medicine time."

They didn't move. I had to say it louder.

"Girls! Bedtime! Brush and move it!"

They got up. Nora turned the TV off and Anna met me in the kitchen for her meds. It made me sick again to even look at her chews.

"You still high?" she asked.

"I wasn't high," I said.

"Are you a drug addict?" Nora said from the living room.

"No. I was just kidding the whole time."

"I knew it," Anna said. "High people feel happy. You looked unhappy."

"I had a stomachache," I said. "I think I ate a bad egg. And high people are not always happy. Where have you seen high people? Oh, the hell with it."

The headache was returning.

"Let's all go to sleep," I said.

By then, I'd realized I'd made a great mistake eating the entire chew at once, that they were meant to be cut up into fifths. They even had marks on the packaging, like butter sticks. But never again, I swore to myself. As the girls headed for their rooms, I made my way to the fridge and threw the "For the parents" baggie into the garbage.

The schools Anna and Nora attended in Bayside were quite close to the house. A benefit of this was that on mornings after a late evening with dance or sports, I could let the girls sleep relatively late, even though that would mean we'd feel rushed once they were up. They had to wash, eat, dress, brush teeth and hair, make sure all their stuff was packed in their backpacks, etc. before hopping in my car.

I'd try to wake them in the way my own mother would wake me when I was a child. I'd speak softly, rub their heads, tell them magnificent things about themselves, how proud we were of our brave, smart, and beautiful daughters. This sweet scene was not intended to drag on very long. We didn't have the time, but it felt right, better than an alarm clock blaring or my yelling from downstairs.

It also gave me the best hope that Anna would emerge from sleep without a seizure. There was no science or doctors' advice behind this approach, but it felt right to me. Nonetheless, every now and then, even after a night of sound sleep, she'd seize right as I gently woke her, and I couldn't help feeling like I'd caused it. I knew she'd head into the day unimaginably exhausted. A doctor once told us that each seizure used as much energy as running a marathon.

One morning, now springtime in her fifth-grade year, I woke Anna up for school, and she went right into a two-minute seizure. It came just as she opened her eyes. When she came out of it in my arms, I noticed something off-looking about her right arm. It hung, not moving like the rest of her body and looked slightly swollen.

"Anna?" I said.

"Yeah..." she mumbled.

"Is your right arm okay?"

"Yeah..."

"Move it," I said.

She couldn't. I put my finger in her palm.

"Squeeze," I said.

She couldn't.

Another ER. And another extended hospitalization. Anna was diagnosed with Todd's Paralysis, a temporary condition some epileptics get after seizures. It can last minutes, hours, days, or weeks. Or longer. The doctors said that it may have been our lowering the Lamotrigine, or just another honeymoon period come to its end, this time with the Colorado CBD. Whatever it was, the seizures were back. She was put on a newer drug called Lacosamide, and a weaning program for the balance of the Lamotrigine. We were also told it was likely that the Todd's had struck in the past but that since she'd only seize during sleep, often late at night, we probably never noticed it. By evening, still in the hospital, full feeling and movement in her arm returned.

I posted the story on Facebook, with a picture of Anna at her softball practice the evening before, then another of her later, giving a shaky smile and wave in the ER. A few days later, a parent of a baseball player I'd coached wrote me after seeing my post, asking if I was interested in exploring bona fide medical marijuana. He was a doctor, and said he could arrange for us to meet someone who could license us to get it in New York, as dispensaries were finally opening. This is how we came to work with Dr. Chin. The hope was that the stuff she dealt with would be stronger than the recreational chews we'd been using. She prescribed Anna a different combination of CBD and THC, with which she'd had success with epilepsy patients.

Reading all these marijuana articles in my office, and recalling how those chews had made me feel that night, I was now convincing myself that cannabis treatment had been an ill-advised idea from the beginning, and that what had happened to Anna over the weekend was exactly what my Aunt Maureen and the others were afraid of.

My cell phone rang again. Dr. Chin. I quickly told her what the doctors at both hospitals said about panic attacks, what I'd observed, what Anna had described, etc. Then I asked if she thought it might all be a bad reaction to the cannabis. At this point, I hoped she'd say yes. It would mean we had both an explanation of the panic attacks and confidence that these weren't seizures of a new pattern. We'd stop the cannabis, withdraw, heal, and never look back.

"I highly doubt it's the THC," Dr. Chin said. "She's taking a very small amount."

"The symptoms just seem to line up exactly with what I'm reading about THC overdose."

"We can discontinue for now," she said. "But did you say Anna felt like she was falling? When these moments came?"

"She said she saw herself falling. Off a car or a ledge or something. And she said she was seeing sharks. Then she told me she saw an alligator last week in science class."

"But when she saw herself falling, she felt like she was actually falling?"

"Yes. The doctors did an EEG and said she's having panic attacks."

"I understand, but those EEGs don't pick up everything, especially in the frontal lobe."

It was the first time I'd ever heard anything like that. I'd always thought the EEGs were the most reliable neurological tests of all.

"From what you're describing," Dr. Chin said, "it's seizures."

After we got off the phone, I walked down the hall and into the classroom. I gave my talk on *The Red Balloon*, then started the movie. I usually sat at the front corner of the room behind the lectern, even when the movies were playing. This way, I had access to the desktop computer and could pause the film to make comments. I could also make sure nobody went to sleep since I'd be facing the students. This time, I went into the hall. I stood there for a good ten minutes, the muffled symphonic music of the soundtrack coming through the walls.

I stared at the blank screen of my phone, as if waiting for something to come out of it, like a genie, who would float up into the air, hover in front of me, and tell me what was really wrong with my child. Maybe he would give me three wishes, like genies do, and I could say, "I wish that Anna never has another seizure," three loud times.

CHAPTER SEVEN

THERAPY

As Dr. Chin suggested, we stopped the marijuana, but Anna continued to show symptoms we'd never seen before. She would shiver every now and then, like she had a chill, jerking her entire body for a second. I read that these were also symptoms of a panic disorder. I had no idea what to think now that Dr. Chin seemed confident this was seizure activity.

At the end of the week, Anna went to hip hop, her favorite dance class. It was an hour long, and she reported that here and there in that time, her heart raced, and her legs felt "mushy." She said she closed her eyes and breathed deeply when this would happen, until it passed. This only reinforced our confusion, since any ability to subdue whatever was happening with breathing tactics seemed like evidence this was anxiety, not seizures.

Anna's face looked ruddy and bloated. At this, Kristen said she wondered if this entire turn of events would eventually be explained by a preteen surge of hormones, which would subside and level out on its own. The first wave of adolescence was arriving, and perhaps if we just rode out the storm, Anna would eventually end up, at worst, back to the usual seizure pattern of previous years.

But she was suffering, and there was little comfort to be had in theories. At this point there were any number of possible explanations, including the syndromes I tried to resist reading about again on the internet. My thoughts were so muddled that I turned to my journal for help.

I had been a personal journal keeper for nearly thirty years. There were piles and piles of marble notebooks, spiral pads, and even some fancier leather-bound diaries in our attic. In addition to my daily activity roundups, reflections, confessions, complaints, rants, outlines for new plays or stories, pleas to the theatre gods, and whatever other gods, there were lists.

My mother was a great list maker. Her theory was, if you're able to see your challenges laid out in an orderly fashion in front of you, you'll feel in control and meet those challenges, item by item. Mine were the traditional types, like to-do lists and pros and cons lists, but also a kind I invented myself: the "How Might This Situation Turn Out and What Are My Chances" list.

Anna's current situation could pan out to be anything from a short-lived fright to a total calamity. I didn't know exactly what to hope for or just how terrified to feel. So I made a list. I broke things down into the possible explanations for Anna's current condition, the efforts in place to address whatever it was, then the hoped-for and hoped-against possible outcomes.

Breakdown of Current Anna Situation:

Possibility 1: Panic disorder
Percentage I think this is the explanation: 35 percent
Probable Cause: Hormones, Stress, Tense house,
    Epilepsy, Genetics
Our Response: Therapy, Calm home, Deep breathing,
    Various remedies

*Bearable Outcome: Anna learns to manage, doesn't
go insane*
*Unbearable Outcome: Anna has worse psychic conditions,
goes insane*

Possibility 2: THC overdose
Percentage I think this is the explanation: 35 percent
*Probable Cause: Medical Marijuana: the THC pill
before bed*
Our Response: Cease use of Medical Marijuana
Bearable Outcome: Full recovery
*Unbearable Outcome: Permanent brain, nerve, and
emotional damage*

Possibility 3: These are daytime seizures
Percentage I think this is the explanation: 29 percent
*Probable Cause: Change in seizure patterns, hormones,
who knows*
Our Response: New med Clobazam, weaning Lacosamide
*Bearable Outcome: Return to original nocturnal seizure
patterns, life as we knew it, which wasn't so great but
not the shrieking nightmare we have now*
*Unbearable Outcome: Clobazam fails, daytime seizures
become way of life, which is no life*

Possibility 4: Some awful syndrome has begun
Percentage I think this is the explanation: 1 percent[1]
Probable Cause: Genetic
Our Response: Doesn't matter

---

1   *Sometimes 99 percent if I am down, or if it's first thing in the morning, and I'm
alone in the shower and the walls are closing in.*

Bearable Outcome: I die a quick death before I see it play out
Unbearable Outcome: N/A

The details of this week certainly had its fresh new features, but it was all familiar too. It was like every other high-adrenaline, confounding scare we'd had over the years. It was battle mode, fight or flight, under siege by our invisible enemy, its purpose to kill our child. My list got me into a better, more constructive mood. I could clearly take stock of what we were trying and everything we hadn't tried yet and take action—like getting Anna into therapy. I started Googling therapists.

I'd had three or four therapists in my adult life. The first two were before I was married, usually as part of an impulse to "fix" whatever the problem must be that caused another relationship to end. But part of me also bought into the cliché that a real New York writer had to have a real Manhattan shrink with whom to discuss the trials of a life of the mind. But since being married, my latest two therapists heard me talk mostly about epilepsy, and trying to preserve some kind of sane marriage around it. It was useful to me, no doubt, but I'd stopped going mostly out of an inability to fit the sessions into my schedule.

Finding therapists for me was always easy. Whatever health insurance I was on would provide a list of covered doctors, and I'd pick one. Child and family therapists, I'd now learn, weren't as easy to find, at least in our area of Queens. We weren't too far from Great Neck, which is known for an abundance of psychotherapists, so I hoped to find someone within a reasonable distance. It took a while. And evidently, the business had adopted some strategies from the online dating industry. I was surprised to find photos and testimonials of the doctors as if they were prospective hotels, restaurants, or singles. Their profiles offered life and career details about themselves and their particular "philosophy." Ironically, all this information made choosing harder, since I found myself judging faces more than anything else, not really buying the personal statements as anything but sales strategy. I wished it was just all names and phone numbers.

In the end, the decision was made easier because most didn't take our insurance. One referred us to a doctor only fifteen minutes from our house. She didn't have a slick website or photo or statement anywhere. I called; she called me back and sounded like what I had always thought a therapist should sound like: sympathetic but down to business. We were fortunate. There had been a cancellation, and a slot was open early the following week. I booked it.

I moved on to the next steps in our response plan to the possibility that this was a panic disorder. I bought an app for my phone called Calm. Then, I went to the drugstore, asked the pharmacist for any over-the-counter anti-stress products and was directed to a magnesium powder product called Naturally Calm. I planned to play the app at night while Anna slept and give her the powder to, as it read on the box, "relax nerves, muscles and blood flow on a cellular level" during the day.

These chores all felt good. Instead of waiting to see if the Clobazam had any effect (which I supposed would be shown by whether or not Anna resumed having only the nocturnal seizures we were used to), or finding out if cutting out the marijuana would help, or relying on the next neurologist appointment for yet another round of EEGs, I was making moves, trying things, looking for a solution. I even started to revisit the diet options—gluten free, paleo, ketogenic, etc. I didn't mention this to Anna. Such thinking definitely wouldn't promote calm in her, but I did research. I wondered if I could find food that adhered to these diets but tasted so good that Anna would never even know. A fantasy, but I wondered.

This had always been the mental and emotional balancing act, the cloak and dagger; the shell game I played on myself. For these few years, her seizures hitting only during sleep allowed us a sense that Anna's life was some version of livable. The seizures would come and go, and we'd fall back to sleep. Our sleep, and our life, could resume, the monster having moved on for the moment. But in times like these, when we were unmoored, disoriented by a new onset of symptoms, there really wasn't any escaping the reality that this had all been nothing but an undeniable nightmare from the beginning.

Beyond Anna's current situation, I also had lots to do. Even as an adjunct, mid-April had always felt intense, with final papers or exams and all the reading and grading I had to get done by the Spring semester deadlines. But now, with the Mercy job, I was learning how things get for a full timer, as the academic year comes to its end and graduation approaches. On top of the classwork, there were college-wide, school-wide, and department-wide meetings, committees, campus events, and open houses. And the theatre club final performance was approaching fast.

It was going to be a lot harder navigating through all my responsibilities at the college with all that was happening, but I tried to keep quiet about it on campus. I told Jay the basics the next time I saw him in the office. He was helpful to talk to, as always, and encouraged me to take whatever time I needed to be at home, but I didn't at all want to assume the role of the brand-new faculty member with the disturbing personal life. Even after all my years at CCNY, only a handful of trusted colleagues really knew about Anna.

One night, as Calm played the lulling sounds of raindrops hitting jungle leaves, as Clobazam, Lacosamide, and water-dissolved magnesium coursed through Anna's bloodstream, she sat up out of sleep in a seizure and fell off the bed before I even moved. She hit the wood floor headfirst, somehow missing the buffer of blankets and pillows I'd arranged. The sound of the impact was bone to wood, like the crack of a baseball hitting a bat. The daze she'd be in after a seizure would normally put her right back to sleep, but this time, the pain woke her completely. She cried hard, holding her head, as I ran downstairs for an ice pack. I held her in her bed, keeping the pack on her brow, where I could see a bump collecting itself. It was near 3 a.m.

"Daddy," she said through short breaths.

"Yes, baby."

"Can I ask you a question?"

"Of course."

"It's a weird question."

She sniffled and shivered.

"Anything. Please, ask it."

"It's about boys."

I was surprised and happy to hear this. A "normal" question. She was in middle school, almost twelve, thinking like kids do, even after however many thousands of seizures, these recent new symptoms, and even after a headfirst crash to the floor.

"Oh geez," I said, teasingly. "Boys!"

Tears still in her eyes, she smiled, as if she knew I'd react like a fool.

"Stop. Serious!"

"Ask me. I know it's serious," I said. "And I think I'm a boy, so maybe I'll know the answer."

She closed her eyes and adjusted the ice pack, then looked up at the ceiling.

"So what's the question?" I said.

"What boy will ever like me, with all this?"

"All of them," I said, gutted. This was the enemy, winning. "All the boys. They will be lining up outside and I will be screaming at them to get the heck home. I will be guarding you until you are... maybe thirty or forty. There will be too many boys liking you."

Anna laughed. It was a genuine laugh, I thought.

"I knew you'd say that," she said.

"You did?"

"But it's okay."

"What do you mean 'but?'"

"It's okay that you're lying," she said. "I think it's okay to lie if you love someone and have to."

I went on and on and she laughed at my visions of her future, a famous dancer with her own famous dance company, a diploma from Mercy College hanging in her room in her splendid apartment, where her father stood thwarting the unfit suitors and monsters. Me, her old, sleepless, stalwart guardian outside her door, or on her floor, if need be.

*

We were now almost a full week since the Cohen's overnights, and it was the day of Anna's first therapist appointment. I cut my screenwriting class a half hour short to give myself a jump on any bridge traffic there might be back to Queens. I ended up parked by the middle school well before dismissal, so I used the time to catch up on some work. I emailed Reeyaz, the student president of the theatre club, giving him our final weeks' rehearsal plan leading up to the performance. I also finalized my material for the night I'd be the faculty member co-host at the college's annual film festival, which was a popular campus tradition. Since I'd done some work in film as an actor and writer, I'd been placed on the festival committee right after I was hired, and aside from soon serving as host for one of the screenings, I'd been in on the film selection meetings across the academic year, which was so fun I could hardly believe it was officially "work."

At dismissal time, Anna came to the car. I hadn't heard anything from the school nurse all day. I could see she still had the bloated face, but she seemed more upbeat than she'd been. This immediately put me in high hopes that the medicinal adjustments were helping, and I became even more energized to start with her therapy.

"How was today?" I asked as we pulled away. "Did you feel anything weird?"

"Yes. The same."

"What do you mean by that?"

"I felt stuff."

"What stuff?"

"The same."

"Can you get more specific, Anna?" I said. "Did you feel your heart race? Your legs numb? What did you feel? Did you go to the nurse's office?"

She didn't answer. I looked in the rearview mirror when we came to a light. I saw her shiver a couple times. Some silence passed as we drove on.

"Ready to meet the therapist?"

"Yes," she said.

"Good! We're heading there now."

"I'm gonna vent all my shit."

It sounded like someone else.

"What did you say?" I said.

"I'm gonna vent all my bullshit."

"Anna, what is *that*?"

"What is what?"

The only time I'd ever heard Anna curse was when she'd repeat back a curse that I'd uttered. Nora did the same. I tried not to curse at home, but every now and then, I sure did. For instance, if I'd asked four times for Nora or Anna to shut the television off, maybe the only way it actually got turned off was when I followed with a louder, "I said turn the fucking TV off!" Every time, Anna or Nora would jump on the chance to say, "Okay! We'll turn the *fucking* TV off!" Then, we'd have the obligatory "Don't curse!" and "But you cursed!" exchange that always ended with the even more laughable, "Don't say what I say!" followed by their "Then why did we turn the TV off?"

But here in the car was unprompted cursing. I looked back again to see if she was waiting for some kind of reaction out of me, but she just looked out the window.

"What's with the language?"

"What language?"

"You just cursed. Twice."

"Sorry," she said, with an ironic tone, as if this question surprised her.

"What's with the 'tude?" I said.

"Whatever. Just drive, man," she said.

"Wow. Let's not talk like that, okay?"

"Whatever."

"Is something wrong?"

"Something wrong?" she said snidely, like I was an idiot. "You think?"

"Why are you acting like this?"

"Ugh. You don't get it," she said, completely sincere. "I need my therapist."

"You *need* your therapist? You haven't even met her yet."

I wondered if she'd told her friends she was seeing a therapist today, and one of them gave her the term "vent my bullshit." I never heard Anna use the word "vent" before. Whatever was happening here, I figured I wouldn't dig in too deep with the tit for tat—we were headed to a psychologist, after all, so I left it at that and stayed silent for the rest of the ride.

The office was classic. It was what I was used to with my own therapist experiences: minimalist, neat, easy on the senses. It had a small sofa, on which Anna made herself immediately comfortable, and two armchairs where the doctor and I sat. The PhD diploma and however many other degrees and certifications hung amid a few understated pieces of impressionist art. The day was bright outside, but in here, all was lit by a shaded lamp beside the sofa. When we first spoke on the phone, I gave the therapist an extensive description of all recent developments and, of course, Anna's history. I'd expected to sign some forms, give a copay, and wait outside in my car while Anna began this new frontier of self-examination, but I was asked to sit in.

On one hand, I hoped Anna would get through the forty-five-minute session without any physical disruption. On the other, if an event had to happen, I thought it might not be a bad thing for it to happen in front of the psychologist tasked to identify the cause and come up with a prevention.

As I sat in the armchair, the sight before me was my eleven-year-old laid out on a sofa across the small room from a shrink. There it was, I thought, a live portrait of parenting failure. But before I could dwell too long in self-recrimination, Anna breezily launched into a sustained bitching session about school, some frenemies in her grade, her sister, and her parents. The same jarring looseness I'd witnessed in the car carried right on.

"My parents are very mean and very strict," she said. "Cruel people."

"How are they cruel, Anna?" the doctor asked. I couldn't believe what I was hearing.

"Well, they're like, 'Anna do this!' and 'Anna do that!' And I'm, like, tired and, like, ugh, shit."

"Anna!" I said.

"Well, are the things they want you to do important?" the doctor continued, unfazed.

"Yes," I said, respectfully. "I think they are."

"No!" Anna said.

"You mean like finish your homework, brush your teeth, make your bed.... That stuff?" I continued. The doctor glanced at me, evaluating. I tried not to wonder what she was thinking.

"Yes!" Anna said. "Or, 'Put your phone away,' or 'Get in the shower!'"

"Yeah, those things are sort of necessary, Anna," I said.

"I know, but all in a row?"

"What does that mean?" I said.

"Like, chill. Give me some time, bro. One thing at a time?"

This had gotten ridiculous, fast. A few days ago, I was in my father's car holding her as she was having what I thought was a heart attack. We were told she had an acute anxiety disorder, and to treat it with psychotherapy to unearth the source of her stress. This was it? Making her bed?

"Don't you think your parents have to teach you those things?" the doctor asked.

"And they never hold hands," Anna said.

That silenced the room for a good ten seconds. Now I was about to get my copay's worth.

"Who doesn't hold hands?" the doctor said.

"My parents."

Another silence.

"Your parents don't hold hands?" the doctor said.

"They don't love each other."

"Anna..." I began.

"They don't hold hands, or kiss, or hug..." Her eyes watered.

"Mommy...and Daddy love each other," I said. "And we love our girls very much."

"And they don't sleep in the same room because of me."

"Anna," I began, but said nothing else.

"They'll get a divorce," she said.

"Nobody's getting a divorce," I said. I turned to look at the therapist. I couldn't really guarantee that, about a divorce, and she knew it.

"You're always yelling and fighting," Anna continued.

"We won't get a divorce."

I wondered if the doctor was finding this the simplest case she'd ever come across: kid made a nervous wreck by two Type A, highly stressed, overworked, befuddled, and scared-out-of-their-wits parents. Poor kid, she must be thinking, no wonder she has panic attacks. This was it, I thought, just hearing Anna say these things. It's a panic disorder, and we caused it.

Something of a crackpot theory about Shakespeare's play had occurred to me some years after Anna's epilepsy lanced into our lives. I thought I knew why Shakespeare ended his comic *Love's Labour's Lost* like a tragedy, with the lovers parting, rather than marrying, as the audience would have expected. Shakespeare's young son, Hamnet, died around the time he was writing it. I imagined the great playwright at his London theatre office, at his desk, working on his new hilarious romcom, probably called *Love's Labour's Won*. Then, a messenger arrives from Stratford, where his wife and children lived. He is flattened at the news, of course. So what does he do? Now that his heart is broken? His marriage was already pretty bad with all the distance, now this. How does he even think about putting a new comedy on the stage? He changes the ending, that's what he does. And the title. Nearly five acts of romantic hilarity, before he brings news of death onto the stage, and everyone ends up alone. The comedy is "Lost."

Hamnet was the same age as Anna when he died. *Love's Labour's Lost* premiered a year later.

That was our marriage, maybe. Love, then labor. Marriage, then a kid. Next, for the unlucky some, it all gets lost. Kristen and I had gotten together in the most romantic and comedic circumstances—a great Hollywood story to tell our friends—and we, for a bit, came to know how to be characters in that kind of plot. But once Anna's seizures came, and with them an everyday sadness, that happy romcom was over. What the hell were Kristen and I, who only knew each other a few young, fun years, doing now? This wasn't what we foresaw when we got married. We had ended up in the wrong play, half hoping every day that the curtain would come down on it.

"Ah, Anna," I said. "Your mom and I do hold hands."

The truth was, Kristen and I did hold hands every now and then, but not like Anna meant. These were moments Anna would never see. How would she? They'd be rolling her away for an MRI, lifting her into an ambulance, or pinning her down for the needles and wires and tubes, as we, her goddamn parents, hands clutched, watched her disappear, from however close the doctors would let us get.

CHAPTER EIGHT

CRUNCH TIME

With my four-course full timer's load at Mercy and the one class at City College, it took serious hustle all year to have gotten the girls from their schools each afternoon, then to dance. Kristen taught too far out on Long Island to be back in time for their dismissals, so I had to get myself back to Queens by 2 p.m. from my morning Playwriting class in Harlem on Mondays and from my morning Oral Communications class at the Bronx Mercy College campus on Tuesdays and Thursdays. We relied on the generosity of a local parent on Wednesdays, when I had to be at Mercy's main Dobbs Ferry campus all day and into the night for more classes and club rehearsals. Kalli lived a few blocks away and picked up Anna and Nora from school with her own daughters, fed them, and brought them all to ballet class. We carpooled on the other nights, since Kristen or I would be back in Bayside to bring everyone home. Other moms and dads played taxi too, all of us helping each other figure it all out each week.

All four of our parents worked full time. Fortunately, Kristen's mother's work as a lawyer gave her the most flexible schedule, and any time a conflict would arise that prevented me getting home at the usual time, Geri could usually manage to get to our house. For the upcoming two weeks, we'd be needing her almost every day. On top of my classes, I had a bunch of obligations. As part of Mercy's community engagement, I was hosting a discussion of Edwin Arlington Robinson poetry at the Dobbs Ferry Library. I was also co-presenting an Argentinian movie at the festival, directing the theatre club show (which was only a week away), and practices for my summer baseball team were starting that weekend. Even without the swerve Anna had taken, this stretch was going to be rough.

It was time for a list.

What Needs to Get Done and How I Will Do It

Commitment 1: Classes—Every day but Friday
Have lesson plans ready at least one week in advance
Get all reading done of student work over the weekend
for Monday class
Confirm Michael's visit to Directing Class next week

Commitment 2: Library Night
Review six Robinson poems
Re-read two critical essays on Robinson
Read my brother Scott's dissertation on the subject,
steal his ideas

Commitment 3: Film Festival
Re-watch the Argentinian movie
Prepare points on the movie's structural innovation
for audience discussion
Read at least three reviews of the film, American and
Argentinian, steal their ideas

Commitment 4: Theatre Club Show
Rehearse Wednesday (before film festival), Friday,
    Saturday, Sunday, after baseball
Tech and rehearse the show in the theatre all day
    next Monday, perform show that night

Commitment 5: Baseball
Think about nothing but baseball for those hours on the field

How I get this all done:
Decide that Anna's episodes will be stopped either by
    psychotherapy, Clobazam, or both
Don't start feeling bad for self

Despite the Clobazam, Anna's episodes continued. We knew we had to have patience. It was still early in its introductory period; too early to judge if it would work. We continued with the magnesium powder, the Calm soundscapes, and deep breathing. At this point, it could feel almost pointless to try to discern whether Anna was having panic attacks or seizures. For all I knew, one caused the other in a vicious circle.

I pulled off the library discussion well enough. I had an adequate grasp of the poems and Robinson's biography to not make a fool of myself. I always enjoyed his writing and always liked that he, an eventual Pulitzer winner, was long a middling writer who had to endure some seriously-demoralizing survival jobs—like checking shale loads for the New York City subway construction and working a desk job at the Customs House. It was the same desk job Herman Melville took at the end of his life, when he couldn't support himself with his writing. I often wondered if those writers hated being asked what they did for a living as much as I did.

The ideas in my brother's paper were helpful conversation points. One man at the library insisted on singing the Simon and Garfunkel version of Robinson's "Richard Cory" for everyone after we discussed that poem. As he sang, quite nicely, really, I snuck a look at my phone, which I'd sworn to myself I'd keep in my pocket. Nothing from Kristen. No texts or missed calls at all. I was so relieved that tears came to my eyes. Everyone thought it was the man's singing.

When I got home, I switched places with Kristen on Anna's floor at about ten. Starting around midnight, she had six seizures. Nearly one per hour. Then it was time to get up for school. She was miserable, naturally, and wanted to stay home, but I, also miserable, made her go in, still numbly holding to the hope that one way or another, this would all still come back to that abnormal normal I now missed so badly. Not that it was anything to really want, but I needed to believe it'd be back, just to get through these days.

The film festival ran all week, but I wasn't hosting until the Wednesday night of my presentation. Still, I gave my Tuesday evening students in the Bronx the night off, so they could attend the other films if they wanted. I also put Reeyaz in charge of that day's rehearsals. This way, I could be near the middle school all day in case anything happened.

After I dropped the girls off in the morning, I kept in contact with Anna's school nurse throughout the day. She checked in regularly with the classroom para. I realized I hadn't had to do this in a long time, to endure the same moment to moment apprehension we felt when Anna started preschool, when the seizures would still commonly come in the daytime. Since then, communication with the school nurses and paras had only to do with how she was struggling with side effects or tiredness, not the possibility that a seizure would happen at school. Any time she seemed "off" in elementary school, her para, Helen, who loved her like she was her own child, would let us know. This was how we'd been able to keep track of Anna's response to new meds or dosage adjustments. It was all tense and upsetting enough, but it hadn't been like it was now. I'd forgotten what this level of constant expectation felt like, but it was coming back to me quick.

At about noon, the nurse said Anna seemed okay, even upbeat, despite looking worn out, which was logical, considering the night she had. She said the rescue med was out of its case and ready on her desk, the same syringe we now had out and ready at home.

"Let's hope it doesn't come to that," I said. "We've never had to use it."

After her first hospitalization at five months old, Anna never had another "cluster" or a seizure that lasted more than five minutes. They'd always been spread apart long enough not to qualify the situation for the Diazepam. Despite each one of the thousands that ever happened being excruciating for her and for us, seizures in a case like Anna's aren't considered "emergencies" in and of themselves, once it's been established that they're going to happen to her no matter what. Only if they start bunching close together, or lasting longer, is it a 911.

That evening, the four of us sat around our small dining room table. This was a rare thing, all of us able to eat together. Kristen had made chicken cutlets, mashed potatoes, and spinach, while I helped Anna and Nora get their homework done early. Anna's occasional cursing continued, but in the spirit of keeping a peaceful atmosphere, we pretty much let it go. We lit candles, streamed some sleepy Bach through a laptop and, as we ate, talked of happy summer plans.

"It's almost here, ladies," I said. "It's gonna be the best summer yet."

Beyond the usual Happy Fourth trip, we discussed how my sister Kaitlin, a school psychologist I had also been recently consulting over the "panic attack" diagnosis, had invited us to stay at the Fire Island house she'd rented for a week in July with her boyfriend. In August, we told the girls, Kristen's sister and her husband were hosting the entire family upstate at their house on Seneca Lake. After that, we talked about the southern road trip we had planned. One of my plays was being done in Asheville, and we'd decided to drive down to attend, then visit some former professors at Wake Forest, stopping in Virginia on the way for a few days at Colonial Williamsburg. I looked at the coming summer as a kind of celebration of this school year with two happy "firsts": my first year at Mercy and Anna's in middle school.

"So it's kind of like time travel," I said. Kristen and I were explaining Colonial Williamsburg.

"The whole place is set up to be like it was just before the American Revolution," Kristen said. "I'm actually teaching my fourth graders about that time now."

"Do they like it, Mom?" Nora asked.

As this was the grade Nora was in, she was often interested in what her mom was doing in the Long Island version of the curriculum.

"They just can't get enough of it, Nora."

"I don't understand," Nora said. "Don't the people in Williamsburg know the war is over?"

Anna laughed. Nora's question was sincere, but she quickly caught on that it was funny.

"Didn't they go to fourth grade?" she continued, pouring it on. "Didn't they notice nobody dresses like that anymore?"

"They're pretending," I said. "It's called a living museum."

"That's creepy," Anna said.

"The people there are acting and teaching the tourists about the history," Kristen explained. "And the buildings are restored to look and feel like they did when it was still an English colony. So it's like you're walking around in the past."

"What is *restored*?" Nora said.

Kristen started to answer when Anna, without warning, vomited onto the table. She made a choking noise, stiffened, and her breath seemed to jam in her throat. One arm flew out and dashed her cup of water onto Nora. Kristen got to her before she fell off her chair. Rosalind barked. Another of the year's firsts.

When she recovered, I helped Anna upstairs and into the bathroom. She showered while Kristen cleaned up the mess, then helped Nora resume her homework. I sat on the edge of the toilet, talking at the shower curtain.

"Anything feel strange?" I said.

"Everything," Anna answered.

"Anything numb or heavy?"

"Fucking everything."

"Do you have to curse?"

She didn't reply. Maybe it was a stupid question.

She was so groggy now that attempting homework was out. About a half hour later, Anna's neurologist answered my email that described to her what had just happened at the table. She instructed us to double the nighttime dose of the Clobazam. I gave Anna the meds, prepared my area on the floor beside her bed, and Anna was quickly sound asleep.

I still had work to do and tried to do it on my phone. I didn't want the light of the screen to bother Anna, so I sat under a heavy comforter in a kind of tent for one. I read some reviews of the movie I'd be introducing in less than twenty-four hours at the festival, wrote emails to Anna's teachers informing them why she wouldn't have her homework done, then to the members of the theatre club, reminding them that we were days from showtime, and to meet with their scene partners to run lines. And I Googled Clobazam, surprised that I hadn't already done it. I found it was a controlled substance, addictive, can affect mood, and along with other side effects, cause suicidal thoughts. Mixed with the Lacosamide she's already on, I thought, who knows what might be ahead. The more meds a person had to take, the greater likelihood that the side effects would be worse.

I turned the phone off at about midnight and closed my eyes but couldn't sleep. I doubted it was the drug warnings I'd just read. I'd seen that kind of thing on every bottle of every med Anna had taken. Maybe it was that there was still so much ahead to get right in the next days. Maybe it was too much cell phone. Maybe it was how awful that seizure at the table was or that I was afraid that if I slept, I'd miss the next one.

At about 3 a.m., I got what I was waiting for. I was still awake when she turned, let out a long, voluble exhale, then shook. It lasted about thirty seconds. This happened about once every hour until 7 a.m. Kristen, ready to leave for work, popped her head into the room.

"About four in the last four hours," I whispered. Her head dropped.

"No way she goes to school," Kristen whispered back.

"She's missing so much," I said.

"Do you want to send her?"

I had no answer. If Anna stayed home, it would be because she'd had seizures for the past few hours and was too beat up to function. We were also clearly no longer limited to nocturnal seizures, so how could she be at school with the possibility of having one there? But then again, despite what I saw with my own eyes at the table the night before, I thought of that social worker, so sure that anything outside the realm of sleep was caused by anxiety and wouldn't be a threat at school. So then, I thought maybe we should send her. If she could make it through the day, it would help her catch up with some classwork. And it would sure help me.

"I can't stay home, Kristen. This is hell week for me."

"I'll call my mother on my way to work," she said. "If she can't get here, I'll turn around and take a sick day."

Nora got up, showered and dressed, unassisted as usual. Kristen had left breakfast waiting for her. She ate alone as I stayed with Anna in her room. This morning, for the first time, Nora would walk the three blocks to her elementary school by herself. She'd long petitioned for this chance, and at last, I gave it my blessing. I had to. I couldn't leave Anna. I texted Helen, Anna's former para, to ask her to confirm for me that Nora arrived at the school, which she did.

Kristen called and reported that her mother could come save the day. Geri had already planned on picking both girls up after school and spending the rest of the evening, but now, she would defer her morning plans and get to me by 10 a.m.

Anna woke up at about nine, and I could finally rush a shower and get dressed. I had her sit on the floor outside the bathroom while I was in there, leaving the door open so I could peek my head out to check on her. She had my laptop, and I noticed she was watching YouTube.

"Whatchya watching?"

"I want to draw a flower," she said. "This will teach me."

"What is it?"

"Art lessons."

"Nice!" I said. I was happy to see her wanting to do something that wasn't watching television or going back to sleep. "Sounds like a great idea."

"My art sucks," she said. Yet another word I hadn't heard out of her before. "Nora's is great. Mine sucks."

"My art *stinks*, Anna."

"Well, I get my art from you, then."

"That's not what I meant," I said.

Downstairs, we waited for Geri. I gave the morning dose of meds, then fried some eggs for breakfast. Anna sat on a stool at the table working on her flower drawing. She was focused hard, following the teacher in the video. I was lifted. Not only was it quickly becoming the most ornate and lovely thing I'd ever seen her draw, but her sitting there, hunched over the pad so engrossed by what she was doing, was how Nora looked when she drew and did her homework. Maybe this was the beginning of the new medicine working, I thought. She's clear-headed, more at ease, comfortable. Maybe we've found the magic pill in Clobazam. With whatever hysteria and sleep deprivation I was suffering, I felt this could be true, even after the night we'd had.

I placed the eggs near her and told her she could eat whenever she was ready. She thanked me, and I began to wash the pan. Just as I finished and shut the water off, I heard the sketch pad slam onto the tabletop. I spun around to find her sitting straight up, staring at me, her face bright red. My first thought was that she'd made a mistake on her drawing and was throwing a tantrum.

"What's the matter?"

She didn't answer, but gulped twice. Her hands tightly held to the side of the table.

"It's doing…it," she stammered out.

I ran behind her, holding her on the stool. She pushed back into me, as if something was coming at her.

"Breathe, Anna, it's okay. Breathe deep."

"I…am," she fought to say.

Her body tension came to a kind of totality, then softened.

"I'm okay," she said softly, winded. "I'm okay."

As fast as it came, it was gone. As if nothing had happened, she reached for her pad and resumed drawing.

"It was like the social worker sort of described it would be," I told Geri after she got there. "She was sitting with her drawing, looking scared and like she couldn't breathe. Then it all calmed down."

"Like a panic attack would be," Geri said.

"I don't know. But the usual part that comes with a seizure didn't happen. Just the tensing up. I'm totally confused at this point. I don't know if it's one, two, or three different things. But whatever it is, I only know it's bad."

"We'll find out, and we'll get her better."

Anna could not be in better or more loving hands than Geri's, but it was hard for me to walk out the door. Every moment since the seizure the night before, I'd been within arms' reach her. But she was happy to see Geri, and the two made plans for the day.

"I'm getting Nora from school at two twenty?"

"That's perfect," I said.

"We'll go and get her together, Anna," Geri said.

Anna liked this.

"And Nora has ballet at three thirty," I said.

Anna, who'd gone back to her drawing, turned to face me.

"I have dance too."

I didn't realize at first that I'd only said, "Nora has..." I had assumed Anna would not be going. Our policy had always been, if you're sick enough to stay home from school, you're too sick to go to dance. But she wasn't "sick" in the typical sense and certainly wasn't faking it, which was the whole point of the policy, but things were so unstable and unpredictable that the exertions of two hours of ballet and lyrical classes seemed an unlikely choice.

"I don't know, Anna."

"I'm going to dance," she said, bluntly.

"Well, I want you to," I said. "I just wonder if we should let this medicine get things under—"

"I'm going."

I saw that this was firing her up, and quickly.

"Okay, okay. Sure," I said. "Calm down."

Geri put her arm around her.

"We'll have a nice, easy day and we'll see how we feel," she said.

Anna seemed assured. She asked Geri to look at her picture. I got out the door and into my car.

For the next few days, it was as if I were both at a play and in one too. I was actor and audience, watching myself closely, while playing my parts. Over the week, I'd played the role of a man having to go before his students, a film audience, a college theatre club, colleagues, strangers...and make no indication that he is steadily becoming convinced his daughter is dying, that she had been dying for years, that of the tens of thousands of people with epilepsy that perish every year in America alone, she was destined to be one of them. In the first act of this play, I introduce to the class our Persuasion unit and the three rhetorical proofs, saying my lines loud and clear as the communications professor. In the second, the film festival, I discuss contemporary Argentinian cinema in the form of an international film scholar. Act three is theatre club rehearsal, where I play director. I urge the actors to pick up their cues and find their light. In the department office, act four, I am faculty again, planning my next semester's schedule with the chair who hired me. My acting is very good in this scene, I find, as the truth is, that I cannot even picture life in the fall. I don't want to. In this play, the way things were going, by next semester, act whatever it would be…things could have become so unbearable that the audience would have exited.

Geri was with Anna every day and reported moments she was overtaken by what sounded like what are known as epileptic auras. People with epilepsy commonly report these strange, even sometimes pleasant spells before a seizure's onset. Even on their three-block walk to get Nora from school, Geri said, Anna had to stop and sit down, describing such a feeling.

During ballet class that first night, Nora had said, Anna's face looked swollen, and her movements were lumbering. She'd left the barre three times to sit and rest. She sat out all of lyrical class. The following night, I returned from campus just as Kristen was bringing the girls home from jazz and tap. We pulled up to the house nearly simultaneously. I opened the door, the three walked past me into the porch, took their jackets off, and began to tell me with great zest that the tickets to the recital had been handed out and that ours were excellent seats. We'd bought many, enough for all the grandparents, ourselves, and more.

"Let's get those to a safe place," Kristen said. "Can't lose those things."

Anna opened her dance bag to fetch the tickets. As I watched her rifle through her things, I saw her twitch once, her shoulder popping up toward her ear.

"Anna, you good?" I said.

"Yes."

"Was that a chill or something else?"

She wobbled back, then adjusted her footing, and lunged toward me. I caught her in my arms and held her as she violently punched and kicked in every direction. Her head repeatedly flew back into my jaw, my teeth slicing into my lower lip. Her bottom half went lifeless as I tasted my blood and felt her urine stream down both our legs. She made whimpering sounds with each chopped, labored breath. We stood there, wrapped tight in the middle of that room, a minute, two minutes, until it passed, and she was out of it, held up only by my arms.

Saturday night, Nora slept at her friend Juliet's a few blocks away. It would be the first of many sleepovers with Juliet over the weeks to come. Anna now required total attention, as we still waited to see if the new medicine would have an effect, and we were grateful Nora would be spared a close-up view of whatever we might be in for. Juliet's parents Freddy and Samantha echoed other local parents, who told us to send Nora over as much and as often as we needed.

I didn't sleep. Just as we had been tallying all week, Anna had about one seizure per hour into Sunday morning. At about 7 a.m., Kristen took my place on the floor, and I headed off for a field on Long Island for my baseball team's first spring practice. On the way, I stopped at a 7-Eleven for the biggest coffee I could find.

Next Level Baseball fielded three teams divided by player age: fifteen and under, sixteen and under, and seventeen and under. From early March through late May, we didn't play games, since the boys would be with their high school teams. In late April, however, we'd begin holding workouts on Sundays for the players who could make it. This morning, all three levels would be practicing together, which was always fun for me since the entire coaching staff, guys I loved being around, would be there.

Manning ran things like a professional spring training. He always brought a highly-organized, specialized, multi-station workout plan, with each of the coaches assigned to run specific field drills. I either threw batting practice or worked with the pitchers. The sun was out, and we expected to get good work accomplished.

The players were stretching and doing calisthenics when the first text from Kristen came.

ANOTHER SEIZURE

It had been well over an hour since the last one, and I knew Anna was still sleeping. The next one, though, came forty minutes later. I was tossing baseballs to coach Mike Ambort, who was hitting groundballs to the middle infielders.

ANOTHER ONE – THIS IS CLOSE TOGETHER

GIVE HER THE MORNING MEDS, I wrote.

ALREADY DID

SHE STILL SLEEPING?

YES

Ambort was in his early thirties now. In his high school days, he was one of the best ballplayers on the Island. He played for Lamar University and the Giants organization for four seasons before arm injuries ended his career. He also knew about epilepsy. He was an EMT for a while, and, I would now learn, his cousin had a son with a case.

"You should talk to Donna," Mike said, after I told him what the texts were about. "Her son seems like he's doing better."

Another text came about an hour later. Three seizures in ninety minutes. We were approaching cluster numbers. If this gap between seizures kept shrinking, we'd have to give the rescue med. I called home.

"We have to keep her awake," I said. "We gotta see if they stop."

"I've had her up since the last one," Kristen said.

Then came a pause. We knew we had a decision to make. Kristen had already called NYU and was told by the doctor on call that if the seizures continued, we had to bring her in.

Neither of us wanted this. Another ER, another EEG, another long wait for contradicting theories, another missed school day tomorrow, maybe even the following day, and more impossible workweek maneuvering for me, for Kristen, and for Geri. And once again, it was a weekend, when things moved even more slowly at hospitals.

"We should take her," Kristen finally said. "I'm scared."

"I'll leave right now," I said, glad she made the decision. I may have just stood there all day.

The moment Kristen and I hung up, I called my parents, and soon they were on their way to our house to help Kristen transport Anna into Manhattan. Freddy and Samantha said they'd hang on to Nora, so I drove straight to NYU from the ball field.

We were brought into the ER area quickly. The place was so crowded with patients that they were administering to people in the halls and waiting areas. This was what a weekend scene could look like in a Manhattan ER, and it was only late morning. Anna had her vitals taken as we sat in a lounge area just outside the double doors of the actual ER wing. There were many other families and patients out there with us—one young man who had hit his head in a rugby game couldn't remember his name. Another was a small child with a high fever. Doctors moved through the room, quickly asking basic questions about why each of us was there. The rugby guy and the toddler with the fever were left in the lounge, but Anna was brought further in, threaded through the crowd and into a partition equipped for an EEG.

It was even more crowded in this area, loud and frantic with the sounds of the front desk phone ringing, crying children, loudspeaker calls of doctor names and codes, and tense family members asking questions. Patients on gurneys and wheelchairs lined the corridor. All the partitioned rooms were occupied, save the one into which Anna was put. Kristen and I stood beside her on the exam bed and waited for the on-call neurologist.

The wait was long and felt even longer because we were so afraid, and because all the motion around us only reinforced a sense of stillness in our partition. Doctors, nurses, technicians, and staff snaked through the overflow of patients as we waited. Each time someone seemed to be approaching our space, I felt that a possible stop to Anna's emergency was upon us, and my adrenaline rose—and each time that person kept walking to another patient, it felt like a grievous letdown.

A nurse finally came in and prepped Anna's arm for a blood draw. She told us that the neurologist who'd be seeing us was currently "on his way down." I'd already written Anna's regular neurologist that we were coming here. I knew she probably wouldn't be at the hospital on a Sunday but might communicate with whoever this doctor was.

"We sometimes see Clobazam take some time to start really working," the nurse said.

Kristen had been giving her a quick synopsis of the last two weeks. What the nurse said wasn't much to pin hopes on, but my heart swelled at it. Any hint of a branch to grab onto, and I was happy to hold on tight. *Clobazam may take more time to work. Clobazam may yet work.*

The young neurologist made it to our room. He introduced himself and told us he'd already been briefed by our usual doctor over the phone.

"I understand you have a clinical appointment here in a couple weeks?"

"Correct," Kristen said.

"We came in now," I added, "because the seizures, or panic attacks, or whatever they are, seem to be coming closer together this morning."

"We'll keep her overnight for a new video EEG," he said.

I told him that we'd just done this two weeks ago, and that Cohen's had forwarded the reports and films to our neurologist here.

"Yes, she told me. She's reviewed them."

"They said these daytime events were panic attacks," I continued.

"They are seizures," he said.

"No, I don't know," I said, quickly, feeling my abdomen tighten. "They said they didn't see seizure activity on the EEG, so…."

Here I was now, a man who barely passed his undergrad biology courses, debating a big-league neurologist. It was, however, as if I was defending our entire future. I needed to keep the idea alive that these weren't seizures, that it was treatable anxiety, side effects, or psychosomatic symptoms, anything but a change in seizure patterns. It could not be that we were at the end of our little bit of luck that these seizures stayed out of her waking life. What he was saying was the thing we always feared.

"In cases of frontal lobe epilepsy, the EEG doesn't always pick up everything," he said.

I remembered that this was what Dr. Chin had said. The EEG could be missing things. All those overnights, all those conclusions based on these readings, and yet they could mean nothing now. When Dr. Chin said this, I tried to dismiss it. Now, I couldn't.

"If the activity is deep, which is likely the case here," he went on. "Certain seizures can go undetected. I discussed the Cohen's reading with your doctor just now. These are definitely seizures."

"Deep activity" was another thing I'd never heard regarding Anna's seizures. I had always understood that the electrical activity was coming from that diminishing problem near the surface of her brain. All the scans she'd ever had confirmed this, or so I thought we were told. Now, the seizures are coming from somewhere deep? And invisible?

"I'm going to order a bolus dose of Clobazam, five milligrams right now," the doctor said. The nurse wrote something down.

"Would you say that we are still in the introductory phase of this med? We still have a chance it will work?" I asked.

"It's possible," he said. "She hasn't been on it that long. But I believe the plan is now to introduce a third medicine."

"A third?" I said, loudly.

"Yes."

This was getting worse by the word. For so many years, Anna had gotten by on one med at a time with tolerable side effects. Within only a couple weeks, her entire reality, our entire reality, was being upended. Two meds were bad enough, but three meds had always been inconceivable. I didn't want to ask anything else, and I guess Kristen didn't either, which was rare.

"The med will probably be Phenytoin," the doctor continued.

She'd never been on Phenytoin. I knew it was an older medicine, and I knew it had far more significant side effects. I remembered typing letters at the periodontists' office about patients on Phenytoin who had to come regularly have their gums surgically reduced because of the overgrowth. That was only one common side effect. There were others.

"Three meds…" I stumbled to say. "Phenytoin. We're talking major side effects, no?"

He didn't answer.

"How do we measure what's worse, the seizures or being on so many meds?" I said.

"At this point, by her quality of life," he said.

The damning sound of that phrase. "Quality of life." Anna, an athlete, a dancer, a vivacious, kind, inquisitive, beautiful child, now to live half-comatose on a massive mixture of mind-numbing chemicals. We had always known that so many epilepsy patients had to exist like this, on drugs that slow the brain down so much that the seizures are suppressed, or so dulled that the person could survive them. Tranquilized. Lobotomized. Whatever life they may have had, the life they were meant to lead, made nearly impossible.

We didn't know it then, but a fateful decision came before us in that crowded ER. We were told that as of that hour, there were no beds yet available up in the pediatric floor. If none opened, she'd sleep there in that hallway partition, with mobile machinery brought in.

Kristen wouldn't have it.

"Let's get her out of here," she said. The doctor, who'd given Anna the extra Clobazam dose, had left the area to start the admitting process. "We are not sleeping here. It's loud, jammed. There's not even a door to close."

I wrote our neurologist. She wrote back right away saying that since Anna had not been doing well at home, that she should be observed here while we introduced the additional med.

"She thinks we should stay," I told Kristen. "She said they'd set everything up down here until a bed opened."

"Forget it," she snapped back. "What's the difference? We're gonna get a meaningless EEG reading, be here for nights on end, and what? Be sent home to pick up more meds from the drugstore. We can watch her at home. We have the Diazepam."

I certainly never wanted to put us in the position to have to use the rescue med, but I thought Kristen was right. I didn't see a reason to have us go through this hospital routine again. There seemed to be one last shred of hope that the Clobazam would kick in, but even if not, we felt we knew what the next forty-eight hours would hold, and we'd rather deal with it at home.

We packed our things and told the desk we wanted to leave. My parents got our cars out of the hospital garage and pulled them up to the exit on First Avenue. Our doctor wrote me again, asking if we'd left. I told her we did, and that we knew it wasn't the hospital's fault the place was packed but that it was just too uncomfortable. She was concerned. A bed may open up at any time, she wrote. I told her we were going home. She didn't want us to, and clearly thought it was a dangerous choice. And it most definitely was.

But if I've learned anything in my life, I've learned that good things often come of bad things. And as things would turn out, that bad choice to leave NYU may have saved Anna's life.

CHAPTER NINE

DIAGNOSIS

A theatre critic named Eric Bentley once compared two kinds of tragic plays of the modern theatre. The first kind comes to a point where one has the appalling realization that life was never what it had seemed. In the other kind of tragedy, the appalling realization is that life is, and has always been, exactly what it seemed. Not long after we left NYU that day, we would come to feel that we were in both kinds of stories at the same time.

It was obvious we were now facing the worst of our dealings with Anna's health since she was a baby. The concept that the Clobazam would start working was getting almost impossible to entertain. Even as we drove home through the Queens Midtown Tunnel, I was fully convinced we'd be headed right back to the ER at some point that very night.

Anna was wiped out. Not only had she seized through the night and morning, she'd just been given the additional med dose. She slept all the way home and went straight to bed, which in this case had to be the living room sofa. There was no way Kristen or I could retire to her bedroom floor for what was left of our Sunday. We both had tons of work to do, and we could keep an eye on her this way. Kristen sat at the kitchen table to do her class's test grading. Nora, returned by Samantha rested and fed, sat across from her doing homework.

I worked on making a detailed schedule for the all-day technical and dress rehearsal for the following day. Our club's show was scheduled for 7 p.m., and we had one full day in the theatre to coordinate the performances with the lights, sound, and scene transitions before curtain time. The Irvington Town Hall Theatre is a beautiful Classical Revival playhouse that was built in 1902, designed after Ford's Theatre in Washington, DC, of Abe Lincoln's assassination fame. Irvington is the town beside Dobbs Ferry, and the theatre's generous manager had offered the Mercy theatre club use of the space. It was a huge opportunity.

This club had been a major part of my debut year at the college, and I had to see it through successfully. It began in the fall as a small collection of interested students and became this full-blown show going up in the next twenty-four hours. They had all worked hard for many months, and their friends and families, as well as my dean, chair, the school newspaper, and other faculty, not to mention a number of people from the local community, would be in attendance. I wanted them to be pleased. I wanted the students to have the night of their lives. This was a large part of what I was hired to do. Here I was on the verge of getting it done, needing utmost energy and attentiveness, and my poor daughter was falling apart.

In the evening, I set up my sleeping space beside the sofa. Anna didn't have too terrible a night. She slept hard until about 4 a.m., when she began having very short five- or six-second episodes, wherein she'd sit up fast, catch her breath, then flop back down to sleep. It was as if a seizure wanted to come, but was cancelled just as it did. One more time, I managed to spin this observation into a sign that the medicine was kicking in. For the third night straight, I didn't sleep, but the shortened seizures gave me just enough optimism to face the day, which came fast.

Kristen and I agreed that Anna couldn't go to school like she was, but since Geri was able to come over early to be with her, I could get to Irvington on time. When she arrived, Geri sat with Anna as she continued to sleep, allowing me to move from the sofa area. I got dressed, and when I was ready to leave, I handed Geri the pills to give Anna when she woke. Then, I laid out the rescue med syringe on the kitchen table and reviewed with her the instructions on how to administer it.

"Marc," Geri said. "We'll be fine here. If anything happens, I know what to do."

"I'm out of body at this point," I said. "I can't really believe I'm going to spend all day in a theatre. It's what I enjoy more than anything in the world, but how can I possibly do that right now?"

"Try to enjoy it," she said. "It's the only way you'll do a good job."

Typically, even a small stage production would have a week before opening for what is called "tech" to drill a show with all its collaborative elements. Even then, a week is never enough. Every show can always use more time. But traveling shows moved in and out of this theatre every week, so we, the club, would have this one day for our tech on the Irvington stage, and the hours would feel even shorter. In one way, this felt like a good thing. Each time I looked at my phone and saw how much later it had gotten, I was relieved. I stood at the edge of the mezzanine in this gorgeous place, something out of any theatre-lover's dream, calling out direction to the actors on the 116-year-old stage and to the sound and light booth operators at the back of the house. I saw this thing we built together take its full shape. The unmatchable magic of this art form I loved moved our practiced performance into live phenomenon. And I couldn't wait to get home.

At seven, the house had a bigger audience than we'd expected. I gave "places," threw on a blazer, ran onstage, and gave a quick speech. I introduced myself as the club's faculty advisor, thanked Mercy College, a host of fellow faculty, the students, and everyone in attendance. I bid them enjoy the show, ran off and back upstairs to the tech booth, as the enthusiastic crowd launched into applause.

As I watched, I checked my phone between scenes, slipping texts to Geri asking how all was on the home front. "We're doing fine," was all I got back. I figured that would be what she'd write, no matter what. Just as my own parents did, she and Bruce always worried as much about Anna's parents' mental health as much as they worried about Anna herself. Geri knew I had to keep myself together tonight.

The students executed beautifully, scene by scene by scene. Voices were clear, cues were on the money, jokes landed, moments of poignancy were held with perfect timing, and the final lights went down to a roar of happiness. Parents had tears in their eyes and handed over bundles of flowers after curtain call. It was a triumphant night. For the students and their families, sure, but for me too, even if I couldn't really feel it. A circle complete. Here I was, a part of their discovery of this new love in their lives, the one I felt so lucky to discover back at Wake Forest, the baseball player stumbling upon Tennessee Williams. It had taken many years of work to get here, to finally witness this undeniable payoff to my jumbled years as an aspiring artist.

But I had to get out of there. I called Geri when I got into my car, which was parked right outside the theatre. I knew Kristen had been home for hours by now, but I wanted Geri's firsthand account of the day.

"We took a few walks," Geri said as she drove. She, too, was on her way home. "We went to the park, then later to pick Nora up from school."

"How did she seem?"

"She was wanting to get out, to do things. She gets bored lying around. She drew more flowers, we watched *The Greatest Showman*. But she really wanted to get out."

"That's a good thing, I guess," I said.

"We would get about half a block when she seemed to fatigue and need to stop. Just like last time. She'd tell me she was woozy, or her legs felt wobbly. So we'd sit to rest and breathe for a few minutes."

"No seizures?"

"Nothing like a seizure. Just these...."

"Maybe the Clobazam is having an effect. I don't know. I mean, this sounds like progress."

"Maybe. I will say she's stressed about missing school," Geri said. "I think she misses her friends."

"Did she go to dance?"

"Yes. I sat in the waiting room. She stayed in the studio, but Nora told me she sat out a lot."

There was some traffic, and the drive took longer than I'd hoped. Anna was asleep in her room when I got home. Kristen lay beside her.

"How was the show?" Kristen whispered.

"All good," I whispered back. "Everyone's happy. I think the students all went out to celebrate."

"Great," she said.

I sat down beside her.

"They had parents there," I said. "And I did everything I could to fight off what I wanted to imagine."

"Which is what?"

"You and I in the seats, watching Anna and Nora in the same show years from now."

"We'll be there."

"Yeah?" I said. "I don't know. I felt like if I let myself imagine it...the opposite will happen. And only be more painful when it does."

"What do you mean by 'the opposite?'"

I didn't answer. Maybe I wasn't sure what I was saying. Anna was lying there on her side, faced away from me.

"I'm so tired," I said. "And it's still Monday."

"She's been like this since she went to sleep. Sleeping heavy."

"Good."

"What about tomorrow?" Kristen said.

"What about it?"

"She wants to go to school."

Anna had already been falling behind for two weeks, and did seem better in terms of seizures since the extra Clobazam dose at NYU. Still, this was a hard decision.

"You're here until afternoon tomorrow?" Kristen said.

"Yeah. I leave around five for my Bronx class."

"So if anything goes down at school, you can get her out."

"I guess."

"My mom wants to come back tomorrow too," she said.

We went back and forth a few times about school, only to straddle the same fence. It was only when I noticed Kristen tipping toward sending her in that I was suddenly sure I wanted to keep her home.

"Kristen, I know these spells today were relatively small, but what if?"

I described what I remembered from the girl in junior high. The gruesomeness of it all, the stares, the laughing....

"This is why the para is there," Kristen said.

"Yeah, but the para can't *predict* the thing. The para reacts. And by then it's too late."

"We can't predict it either," Kristen said. "We can't keep her home for the rest of her life."

"She's eleven years old. Imagine her knowing all those kids have seen her have a seizure? Imagine that embarrassment? She'd never be treated normally again. Maybe it's just not worth it."

Kristen motioned for me to be quiet. Anna stirred, then got still again.

"Maybe we wait a little longer," Kristen said.

"I don't know what to do," I said.

We agreed we'd see how she slept and discuss it in the morning. Kristen headed to "our" room as I took my place on the floor.

The night went well. For Anna, anyway. She sat up once like she was about to seize—her heart rate was fast, she was breathing hard, but then went back to sleep. Right about when the morning light started, I think I slept a few minutes. Anna woke me up at seven, tapping my shoulder and wanting to go to school.

She lowered the window as I pulled the car to the curb near the main entrance. Anna was looking around at the faces of the other arriving students, coming from each direction on the city sidewalk. She didn't say anything. She smiled but in a way that seemed sad. It was as if she were returning from an absence far longer than it had been. As she opened the door and left the car, her eyes were turned up at the school building, taking it in as if it was the exciting first day of middle school all over again.

I called the school nurse.

"We'll keep checking in on her," she said. "Ms. Lee and all the teachers are on their guard."

"Thank you. She really wanted to be back today."

"I just saw her pass by with friends. She looks great."

For the next four hours, this was the late April Tuesday I had long looked toward as the day I'd be "over the hump." The club show was done; the film festival and library event were done. Classes were in their final gallop. My gratitude that I hadn't yet heard from the nurse reinforced the sweet sense of the semester's end. I wondered if Anna was feeling just fine, at last, stabilized by the Clobazam. I pictured her sitting in class, looking up at the board, taking notes. She was at lunch, eating and chatting with her companions. She was laughing in the halls. Clobazam victorious.

I flipped through my monthly planner—the book from Staples that my colleagues and students teased me about. It seemed everyone now kept their calendars on their phones, but after years of needing to be so many different places every day, I had to see my whole plan each week, each month, on paper, and writ large. I opened to May and found it blissfully sparse compared with the pages before. Next week, I'd bring Anna to NYU to see her neurologist. The Phenytoin addition could wait, I thought, if things stayed quiet. The following Saturday, there was a softball game. I'd bring her there, I said to myself.

The weeks would be thinner, but I did have some important stuff approaching. There were the final papers and exams, Mercy's Commencement, the dance recital, and the appointment Kristen had gone ahead and made with the neurologist whose name we had from Julie at the studio. Her name was Dr. Srishti Nangia at Weill Cornell Medical Center, part of NewYork-Presbyterian.

All of this was still ahead, but then would come June. All I'd have is baseball and Anna's twelfth birthday.

Geri called. She was headed to our house. Kristen was supposed to get back before I had to leave for my class, but Geri had made plans with the girls to make dinner together. She asked if I'd heard anything from the school.

"So far, nothing," I said. "I'm hoping to hell we've turned a corner."

"I'm running early," Geri said. "If you want to head to work, I can pick the girls up."

This would be luxurious. I often arrived to every one of my classes just as the bell rang, so to speak. If I could have a few hours to myself, I could plan the rest of the semester's classes. The faculty office at the Bronx Mercy Campus was a bright, quiet space to get work done.

"That would be amazing," I told her. "Thank you."

"I'm about forty minutes away," she said. It wasn't even noon. "Go do what you need!"

I packed two briefcases, got changed, and drove off. I turned on 1010 WINS. They were talking about the Mets, who were off to a strong start, as they normally were in April. I passed the diner on our corner. I made a left at Dunkin' Donuts. I turned onto the Clearview Parkway. There was no traffic ahead as far as I could see.

A pleasant few minutes, and the last of a way of life.

The phone rang.

"Mr. Palmieri," said the school nurse. "Anna had a seizure."

"I'll be right there," I said.

"She's sitting up now," the nurse said. "She's here with Mrs. Kelly."

"I'm five minutes away," I said.

I was at least fifteen, maybe twenty, but I got to the school in five.

"NYU can't guarantee they'll have a bed," Kristen said to me over the phone.

She was in her car on the way from Long Island. We agreed we were headed to the hospital as soon as she got home. The only question was which one.

"NYU is just being honest," I said. "We may wait for a room, but it's not like they won't see her right away! And anyway, you're asking them to reserve a bed when we haven't even been admitted!"

"I'm calling Presbyterian."

"Kristen, all her records are at NYU. Her doctor is at NYU. I don't think an emergency situation is the occasion to change doctors."

And this was an emergency. In the half hour since I'd arrived to get Anna at the nurse's office, she'd already had another thirty-second episode, her body going rigid, her lips turning blue. After that, she'd had a few of what seemed to be the upper body shivers I'd seen before.

"NYU said they'd keep her in the ER until a bed would be ready," Kristen continued. "I don't want that."

"We know nothing about anywhere else!" I said, raising my voice. "All we have is an appointment scheduled with someone you heard about at the dance place! Now's not the time!"

She hung up. I shared the dilemma, or at least my angle on it, with Geri, who was sitting with Anna on the sofa.

"Marc, maybe it's a good idea," she said. "A new set of eyes? They all communicate anyway, doctor to doctor, I'm sure."

"I don't know," I said. "Someone else just please decide. I can't think."

"Relax, Daddy," Anna said, in a sapped, drained voice. "I had a seizure in school and everyone saw."

"No, they didn't. Ms. Lee got you into the hall before anyone could tell."

"All I remember is standing up," she said. "Then the nurse's office."

The nurse told me what had happened. Anna's para reacted quickly when she saw Anna stand up out of her desk chair in the middle of a lesson. She'd stood so fast that the desk got knocked a few inches to the side. Ms. Lee slid down the aisle, took Anna by the hand, and moved her out of the classroom.

"Nobody saw anything, Anna." I pictured the girl in my middle school. I saw all the faces as they followed her being carried out. I couldn't be sure what Anna's classmates saw or didn't see, but there was no point in being honest about it.

"All they saw was you walking into the hall with your para," I added.

"Ms. Lee's so nice," she said. "I miss my friends."

Another jolt shook her. Then another.

"Just breathe, Anna," Geri said, wrapping her arms around her.

Anna's eyes widened and rolled back. Her face went bright red, and both legs kicked out. I took her from Geri's arms, holding her head against my chest. A third seizure in under an hour.

"Geri," I said, iced. "Please grab me the syringe on the kitchen counter."

Anna jolted again.

"D-Daddy. I f-feel like I'm...I'm...I'm...being...el-e-c-tro-cuted."

She was spasming across her body, as if bombs were going off inside her.

"D-Dadd-Daddy.... Help."

Geri handed me the syringe.

I'm the kind of person who skips reading directions. It was a problem in school, one of the reasons I often had bad grades. I didn't have the patience, or the attention span. My whole life, I thought I could just go straight to the questions on tests, or start plugging in wires of a new appliance, or fastening the pieces of some IKEA furniture we bought. Most often, this tripled the time it took to accomplish a task. I'd known this about myself, and so I'd read the directions that came with the syringe a couple times a year so that if the moment ever came, I could skip them and still get the awful deed done right.

I removed Anna's pants and applied the lubricant solution to the tip. I twisted the top, hearing a click, indicating it was ready.

"I'm...shaking...Daddy."

I inserted the tip of the syringe and pushed. Anna's jolting didn't stop completely, but it eased after a breath or two. Her eyes stared at the ceiling. I dropped the thing to the floor, and crawled onto the sofa beside her, taking her into my arms.

"We're going to the hospital, Anna," I said. "We're going to the hospital, and I will be right there, and they will take care of you."

I put my hands on her head, which lay still upon my chest. I remembered a picture someone had taken of the two of us when Anna was a toddler. We were in a hospital. It was New York-Presbyterian. Or Booth Memorial. Or maybe it was Lenox Hill. Or NYU. Or Cohen's. Or Flushing. Or Northwell. Or Huntington. Or Winthrop. Or Long Island Jewish.... In the picture, I was in the bed beside her, holding her just as I was now. I was looking away, maybe out a window, but Anna was looking at the camera. Her eyes were bloodshot and heavy in the photograph, colorful wires sprung from her headwrap.

"Mommy's almost home, and we're going to the hospital. Breathe, baby. Keep breathing. Keep breathing."

"Pl...please...Da...Daddy," she uttered, barely audible. "No... no...no more."

We brought Anna outside when Kristen pulled up to the house. She and Geri would drive straight to the hospital while I packed a bag and waited for Nora to be dismissed from school.

"I called Dr. Nangia's office," Kristen told me. "She's not in today, but they put me on with the director of Pediatric Epilepsy. I told him I had booked a consultation with Nangia; that she hadn't seen Anna yet but that I wanted to bring her in now."

I didn't have the energy to argue. NewYork-Presbyterian it would be. I buckled Anna into the back seat, as Geri got in and sat beside her.

"His name is Dr. Grinspan. He said to bring her to the ER and that he'd meet me there."

"I'll call my parents and let them know," I said.

The car pulled off. I turned and headed into the house. I walked inside. The sofa was a wreck. The cushions were half off, a blanket was thrown to the floor, a pillow sat jammed in the armrest, where Anna's head had been. The television was still on. *The Greatest Showman* again. Hugh Jackman, as P.T. Barnum, was in a bar, brooding over some evident career failure. A man who worked in his burned-down circus walks over and tells him to stop feeling sorry for himself. Then the other circus people come in and do the same. Jackman stands up and sings, hitting some serious high notes, about making a comeback. Everyone who had been despairing was suddenly over the moon, drinking, dancing, singing, like there was no question the showman's mood swing meant that all would turn out fine. If I had a baseball in my hand, I may have fired it through the screen.

Still, I watched until the song played out. It took a few moments to find the remote. It was buried in the blankets on the sofa. I turned off the television, headed upstairs, and started to pack. It was a good ten minutes or so before I made my first call to Geri and Kristen in the car. I was mechanical as I dialed, detached somehow, as if expecting to hear something distant, like some stranger's story on the radio.

It was as close as I could bring myself to being ready to hear that Anna was dead.

CHAPTER TEN

"HER ONLY CHANCE"

Being someplace, some other place, and no place all at once, was a familiar state of mind by now. So many times during Anna's life, as an emergency played out in all its hot chaos, workaday life had to proceed. In class on a campus, at rehearsal in a theatre, in the waiting room of an audition studio, or where I was now, on the sidewalk outside The Crocheron School, P.S. 41Q, waiting for Nora's dismissal, life for everyone but us seemed to go on, enviably, as usual.

I looked around almost fascinated. How could these two dads to my left be talking about the Yankees; these mothers in front of me talking about graduation pictures? How can the one behind me be speaking on the phone about a real estate listing? How could any of this be while Anna is in critical condition? These weren't original musings. They were King Lear's, and I suppose I was trying to keep myself mentally distracted on that sidewalk by trying to remember the particular lines. They were from Act Five for sure, near the end of the play, gasped in agony by the king as he holds his dead daughter in his arms. He wonders aloud how a horse, a rat, or anything could be alive, now that his daughter wasn't. It was a line that made such sense right now, as the world went about its business.

In my parked car a block away was my bag, packed for the overnights I assumed were ahead at the hospital. I stood frozen among the moms and dads, watching the school's side exit through which teachers led their classes, releasing each student one by one once eye contact was made with a corresponding parent.

A warm, bright day. Bird songs and warm breezes through leaves were suddenly washed under the manic, gleeful shouts of children sprung free from their classrooms, imploring their parents to let them have at the playground across the street. Nora, I knew, would want that, and I would have to say no. She would wince and whine for the friends she was missing on the swings and slides and monkey bars and even with all that lay before me tonight, I felt sorry for her.

"How's Anna?" I heard Kalli's voice behind me.

I wasn't ready to answer.

"Things...took a bit of a...turn," I stammered out, awkwardly. Her hand went to her stomach. "We're in a...we don't know."

"I'll take Nora," she said. "I'll take the kids to the park, then home. Go where you need to be. We've got Nora. Whatever you need."

I stood there, blanked. Kalli ran one hand through her hair and looked away, as if to collect herself. I said thank you. She shook her head as if to say, "Why are you thanking me? What are you standing here for, when you've got us, the McKeens, the Thomases, Webers, Castellanos, Castracanes, Piergrossis, Soulantzoses, Byrnes...and all the rest of your friends here, who've prayed that this day never comes."

I ran to the car and called Kristen the moment the engine was started. I drove toward the Long Island Expressway.

"We took the bridge," she said. "The expressway is stopped, and I didn't want to be in the tunnel."

I still felt NYU was the safer move.

"Are you sure about this, Kristen? We'll be starting all over at..."

"Head of the whole department picked up the phone, Marc, and we've been talking all the way in."

My first thought was that Kristen was grossly mistaken about whomever she had on the phone. In all the years with so many hospitals, I don't think we ever called one and got an actual doctor on the phone. Not this fast, anyway. One calls you back after a few minutes, but sure as hell not a director of anything. It's a receptionist, then voicemail, then maybe a doctor "on call," who would advise very generally, at best.

Now, my second thought was that whoever this Grinspan was, this world-renowned scientist at this peerless institution, based on my wife's call from her car, must have immediately recognized Anna's situation as so dire that it warranted even himself to come barreling down from whatever corner office he worked in and into the bedlam of the ER front lines.

Then, my third thought: Kristen was exaggerating in order to have me stop urging NYU.

"Kristen, I don't think program directors at major Manhattan hospitals suddenly pick up the phone on a random call and agree to escort a new patient inside. As we know well, it can take months to get an appointment with these people."

"He said he was able to bring up Anna's original scans from when she was a baby. He said he'd be there waiting for me, and they'd have a bed for her."

Dr. Zachary Grinspan. Director of the Pediatric Epilepsy Program at Weill Cornell Medicine and the NewYork-Presbyterian Komansky Children's Hospital at Weill Cornell Medical

Center. Professor in Pediatrics and Population Health Sciences. Yale, Einstein College of Medicine, Yeshiva University. Major hospitals, publications, grants, studies....

Kristen was right about the expressway. It was moving slowly enough to read long and wildly-decorated biographies on the hospital website with my iPhone. Dr. Grinspan's headshot was casual, almost in repose, smiling warmly, like it was in a play-bill for some low-stakes community theatre production of a Neil Simon comedy. He looked like he was in his early thirties or younger. I knew this was impossible based on his graduation dates, but that's how he looked.

He had already gone to alert the ER that we were on our way, then called Kristen back after viewing Anna's old MRI scans. She told me this was why she avoided the tunnel: to keep reception clear and stay available for his calls.

"Hi...hell...hello, Dad," I heard.

"Anna," I said. My voice hoarse.

"I'm...it...won't...st...stop."

"We're gonna stop it, baby," I said, loudly.

I heard Geri repeat what I'd said.

We ended the call to make sure Grinspan wouldn't go to voicemail. My car crawled forward as I cursed every foot of the LIE, which stretched ahead like a straight and endless useless runway.

By the time I parked the car in a garage on East 60th Street and sprinted to the same ER entrance we'd carried Anna through over ten years before, the transfer to Critical Care had been initiated. Kristen texted me to change course, not to enter by the ER but rather through the hospital's main entrance, get to the PICU, and wait. In the main lobby, I stood in line to show my identification at the entrance hall security desk.

I passed new mothers leaving with their new babies, food delivery guys, doctors, nurses, and techs coming and going in scrubs, lab jackets, dresses, and suits. I passed family members visiting someone, looking happy or looking terrified, or looking lost. There was the smell of food from the café, tucked around the corner. The ten years since our first time in this place felt erased.

I took the elevator up to the fifth floor, and when the doors opened, I realized I remembered exactly what turns to make along those same colorful New York City-themed walls. I stopped in the hall by a waiting lounge outside the double glass doors that sealed the unit, where a few people sat watching a mounted television. I texted Kristen and Geri to ask if they were inside the PICU yet. No answer. I figured they were in transit, in elevators or halls with no cell service, and, breath by breath, I fought off the thought that they weren't responding because something calamitous had already happened.

After ten minutes or so, I walked to the PICU's double glass doors and pressed the pad of the identification card reader. The doors clicked loudly and slowly swung open. Two nurses and a security guard sat at the reception area. I tried to look straight at them when I gave Anna's name, only at them, nothing else, remembering too well what unbearable suffering loomed here in every direction.

"I don't think they've brought her up yet," one of the nurses said, looking at a computer screen. "I can bring you to the room she'll be in."

I was led to a large room overlooking the East River. It may have been the very same one we were in years ago. A nurse's station was at the front, positioned to observe four corner areas, each outfitted for a patient. Two were currently occupied, curtained off. Ours was near the window. When I got to the far corner, the empty space where Anna's bed would be, two nurses were setting up machines and an IV pole. A technician was readying the monitor and wires of an EEG. I looked at my phone. My sister Brianne. She worked near Lincoln Center at Macaulay Honors College.

HOW'S ANNA?

DON'T KNOW ANYTHING – WAITING IN PICU – NY PRESB 68th ST

COMING

A muffled cry of a small child came from behind one of the spaces in an opposite corner. Then a high-pitched cough and a woman's weeping. She began talking lovingly, gently like a quiet song.

"Shhh. *Mi bebé, Mi bebé especial,*" she said. The baby's cough came again, muffled now, as if the woman had held its head against her. "Shhh, *mi ángel...*"

As I had made my way here, from the sidewalk to this window, through the beeps, loudspeaker calls, trays of supplies, and wheeled machinery being pushed, I had been reminded of my first impressions of this place, where sorrow strangely dwelled with comfort. With that mother's voice behind the curtain in the corner, I remembered that from here, whether one stays an hour or a month, a parent leaves irrevocably changed.

Anna saw me the moment they steered her gurney into the room from the wide hallway. Flanking it was Geri, a PICU floor doctor, and a nurse pushing the bed from behind Anna's head. They'd put her in the gown already.

"Hi Daddy," Anna said, matter-of-factly, like we'd just bumped into each other in the living room at home, on a boring day.

"Hi, honey."

The room's nurse came from her station to our corner as they rolled Anna into place and locked the wheels. The technician began to fix protective pads to the bedside bars. I noticed a white cotton blanket folded at Anna's feet, and just as I reached for it to drape it on her, a seizure struck. Her eyes shot up toward the ceiling and she kicked the blanket out of my hand.

I moved quickly to her upper torso, put my arms around her, and held on. Her legs kicked and kicked, her upper body twisted sharply to her right, lurching against the pad on that side. After a minute or so, she moaned painfully. Geri and the nurse went to help me, as Anna urinated onto the bedsheet.

As the seizure relented, I saw that the privacy curtain had been pulled around our area. I pulled Anna up. One nurse quickly began to gather fresh sheets as another began to remove the soaked ones and spray clean the bed. I moved with her to the other side, where a chair sat, and leaned over the padded bar to get a better position to keep Anna off the bed. I could feel my lower back muscles nearly tear, my lower spine feeling like it would snap. At this awkward angle, with all my strength, I got her up out of the bed and into the chair. I could feel sweat on my forehead. Anna laid her head back into my hands as I stood behind her. I heard Kristen's voice from the other side of the curtain.

"Here?" I heard her say. She entered with a man dressed in civilian clothes, who I realized was Dr. Grinspan.

"Did we get the IV?" he said immediately.

The nurses, wrapping the new sheets around the bed, told him she'd just had a seizure. He looked at me.

"Hi," I said.

"Hi. Zach Grinspan. You're Dad?"

"Yes. She just had a seizure," I said. A nurse held out a new gown. I removed the one she was in and began fitting her into the new one.

"My eyes hurt," Anna mumbled.

"Okay, let's get her back on the bed," Grinspan said. He walked toward me, rolling up his sleeves. "Ready?"

"Yes," I said.

He moved opposite me, reached under Anna's arms and began to lift her legs. He leaned backwards, and we got her over the side bars and lowered her down. He gave an order for an IV of some kind, and another nurse began to prepare the top of Anna's left hand.

"We have to stop this cluster," he said. "That's the first thing. I looked at her scans from 2006."

Anna went into another seizure. The nurse pulled the IV needle back from her hand as Kristen and Geri now stood at Anna's side and held her down. The PICU pediatrician came in through the curtain. He stood with Grinspan at the foot of the bed, watching Anna.

"How long between?" Grinspan asked, his voice slightly raised.

"About four minutes," one of the nurses said, looking at her wristwatch.

Anna flailed again and made a gurgling sound, red in the face, eyes wide. I watched the doctors watching her.

"You've lived with this for so long," Grinspan said.

I thought it was a strange thing to hear, in the circumstance. It was as if in this moment, he let himself reveal an emotional acknowledgment a doctor normally wouldn't, in the midst of a fluid emergency.

"Yes," Kristen said. She was crying. Grinspan looked at me.

"We need to do an MRI soon as we get her stable," he said.

"Okay."

"I think we are going to see a lesion, and I believe I'm speaking prematurely, but I think I'm right," he continued. "We will see the lesion, in the front left, and I think it'll be clear that…at this point…."

He hesitated, as if he was about to say it one way, but now wanted to say it another way.

"I think it's time we step it up."

"How?" I wanted to say, but I couldn't. I didn't want to hear it.

"I'm ahead of myself," Grinspan continued. "Dr. Nangia told me not to get ahead of myself and push for surgery."

I felt my jaw try to drop, but it wouldn't since I was grinding my teeth.

"We haven't seen Dr. Nangia yet," I said, my head reeling, thinking that I could slow this down. "We had our first appointment scheduled for—"

"I just spoke to her," he said. "She's at a conference and will be back in a couple days."

On day one, all those years before, it was explained to us that in the treatment of epilepsy, medication comes first. One tries, then tries another. Then, another. Then, mixes it with another and another. If medication had any chance at all of controlling a child's seizures, or if the child might outgrow the condition, the risk of surgery would not be taken. And so one tries yet another.

But they won't find a lesion, I thought. Dr. Merchant, right here on this floor, had said the same thing he just did, when Anna was months old, based on those old, outdated, misread MRI scans. But later we learned it was something else. There is no lesion. I wanted to clear things up right away.

"Doctor, they ruled the lesion out a couple years after the MRI you just saw from 2006," I said, eager to have him understand that this re-diagnosis was the best news we'd ever gotten about Anna's epilepsy. I told him we understood that if there wasn't a lesion, it meant whatever was in her brain causing the problem could be diminishing on its own, year after year, until eventually, it could be gone. That's what the newer scans had shown. That's what expert radiologists had said. There was no lesion to have surgery for, so discussing surgery wouldn't make any sense. Not for a minute should we talk about—

"I think that's wrong," he said. "I think it's a lesion, and it's wreaking havoc."

"She's had two MRIs since then, and the latest didn't even show anything abnormal. A couple doctors felt these were panic attacks."

I felt as if I were begging him to change his thinking.

"Sometimes, different MRI machines pick up, or fail to pick up, different things. We'll see. We need to get her stable for a scan. These aren't panic attacks. I can tell you that."

The nurse inserted the IV.

"We were always under the impression that surgery wouldn't happen unless there was nothing else possible," I said. If there was some kind of plug to pull on this scene, I would have pulled it. *Surgery.* I didn't want to hear the word again, ever.

"Your wife has told me all the things you've tried," Grinspan said. "If it's what I think it is, and where I think it is, going in to get it might be...her only chance."

I looked at Kristen and Geri. I assumed they were as wildly terrorized as I was that this was even being discussed. I assumed they had already, as I had, pictured Anna on an operating table, skull split open, for the unthinkable measure of brain surgery, awakening, if she ever woke at all, damaged, changed in a way that I knew nobody, doctor or otherwise, could predict.

I expected Geri to stand up and declare, "Absolutely not. Brain surgery is not happening." Geri, who always healthily doubted modern medicine, who researched and scrutinized every pharmaceutical we were ever prescribed, never confident in any of them. Every few months, another alternative herbal remedy, name of some holistic doctor, nutritionist.... She had so much studied skepticism of whatever doctors came up with. Now, she was sitting there, listening to this without protest? Brain surgery? The ultimate "western" option? Where were Geri's, where were my wife's, cries of "Not that! Never!" that were loud and clear inside me?

They kept their eyes on Anna, their arms across her body, their hands stroking her hair, her face, her arms. I looked at Anna's head, the very first of her I saw when she came into the world. I looked at her pale, slightly freckled skin, which ran pristinely up her forehead, draped off the left and right by her long, beautiful hair. A technician I hadn't noticed leaned in and began to pull it back and into braids, to make way for the EEG leads.

Grinspan stared down at his patient. The smile in his headshot nowhere now. After a long moment, he began to order more drugs to be delivered by IV to stop the seizures.

That night, unless it was a violent one, it was hard to see when Anna was in a seizure and when she wasn't. I watched the EEG lines, the information from which was also being analyzed by specialists from somewhere else in the hospital. A video camera overhead recorded her, so the onlookers could compare the EEG reading to her physical movements. Some of the attacks were minutes long, with a lot of movement, while others would emerge as what appeared to be a hiccup or mild irritation. The MRI would not be possible without her being completely still, but there was a limit to how many meds could be introduced, then increased, in a certain period of time to get her that way.

In the blur of it all, I tried to follow the drug names that were being delivered into her: Phenytoin, Lorazepam, Levetiracetam, Oxcarbazepine...then would come the Lacosamide and the Clobazam she was already on. She had never been on this much at once. I wondered if anyone in the world had. Still, they were failing to stabilize her. There was nothing to do but wait for results of the latest increase.

Anna said she was seeing double. The floor pediatrician suggested it was either an effect of the strain of the seizures on her eye muscles or the numerous medications being streamed into her blood. She would doze off between seizures, while technicians continually checked her vitals.

In the hours after we were admitted, a number of people came to see us. After my sister Brianne arrived, my sister-in-law, also named Kristen, who was an assistant principal at a high school near Lincoln Center, and my sister Kaitlin both came right after school hours. My brother Jon and two more of my sisters, Jillian and Maria, came in from Long Island, while my brother Keith drove in from his job as a middle school dean from Staten Island. Bruce arrived with my parents.

"You've got a big family," one of the nurses said. "Beautiful."

Eight siblings. I'm the oldest. Kristen has four. Hers lived spread across the country but were keeping in constant contact through Geri and Bruce. Some of Anna's friends and their parents were already showing up. The girls' dance teacher, Annmarie, Helen from the elementary school. Our corner by the window was jammed.

Dr. Grinspan returned two or three times through the afternoon to report that he'd been keeping Dr. Nangia posted and that it was possible we'd have to put Anna on a steroid if the meds continued to fail to subdue the seizures. He explained that the lesion area was most likely inflamed, possibly irritated by hormonal changes or a growth spurt, that cortical dysplasia patients often experienced a seizure pattern change around this age. When he said this, so sure it was a lesion, I wanted to remind him again that there was no lesion. We would attempt the MRI tomorrow, he said.

It tortured Kristen to leave, but we agreed I would be the one to stay over. We wouldn't hear anything new for the night, and she needed to get Nora home and back to school in the morning, then call for a substitute teacher for her own classroom. As for me, talking with everyone who'd come to see us, doctors or visitors, maintaining that bizarre state of being collected and hospitable while at the edge of emotional breakdown, waiting all those hours for the doctors to turn into our room with some kind of update, had me so tired, I thought I might actually fall asleep when everyone was gone.

I didn't end up sleeping much, but my body felt better lying down on the foldout chair beside Anna. Rather than closing my eyes and attempting to drift, I watched the streams of the EEG lines reflected off the window, pushing across the dark glass, spiking up, down, up, down...and just as I would from the floor in her bedroom at home, I sat up to check her any time I heard even the slightest noise. I lost count at twenty visible seizures.

There was nothing for me to do but hold some part of her... her hand, her arm...when the seizures came. At some point, I pulled my phone out of my pocket and texted Jay at the college to tell him my daughter was in the hospital. I asked him if he could cover my class tomorrow in case I couldn't get to campus. I realized then that I had gotten my days mixed up, and that I didn't have to be there anyway. I thought about writing a post on Facebook to ask for the customary thoughts and prayers. But I left it alone. It was late now, I thought. Why send such ugly news, at this hour, to all those people in my life who still expect some rest come nighttime?

I kept my very-much-awake mind on a small handful of specific things. First was alerting the station nurse to each seizure, in case she hadn't already noticed by hearing the heart monitor blare. She would come to the bed, reset the monitor, time the seizure, and make notes on a chart. In between, I wrestled with the anxious expectation that once an MRI could be taken, once Grinspan and whoever else would see for themselves that this was in fact not a case of a cortical dysplasia lesion, they would bring the thinking back to what I'd begun obsessing about at Cohen's weeks before, that all this was the start of Lafora Disease, or some other unstoppable Doomsday syndrome. Whatever it would turn out to be, however this would end, I was convinced that the days of epilepsy being limited to a part-time menace in her life were over.

The other thing I kept my mind on, or tried to, was the small television monitor mounted on the ceiling, just beside the black plastic eye of the video camera that coordinated with the EEG. Each corner of the PICU room had one. By the remote that extended out of the many wires of the wall behind us, I kept us tuned to a kind of nature channel, which broadcast nonstop, shifting scenes of pleasing waterfalls, rolling plains, and windy grasslands to the sound of soothing instrumentals. It helped drown out the noise from the rest of the floor, which, despite having dimmed its lights in the hallway and corner rooms, carried on with all its activity as if it were high noon.

The EEG machine was on a stand at the foot of Anna's bed, and every now and then, a technician would appear, fiddling with its dials. I would watch his face, lit in a greenish glow by the screen. I'd stare at him, reading into his reflective, coldly-focused eyes for some kind of clue. There was nothing to read, of course. His job was to make sure the machine was working all day, all night, and had surely long ago learned to keep himself impervious to whatever those squiggling lines might be saying about the fate of the patient before him on the bed, hooked to the other end of the wires.

I wasn't sure what time it was when the first member of the Neurology team arrived in the morning on the rounds. Through the night, Anna had different med doses given at scattered hours, as each had to be given twelve hours from the previous dose. Since new meds were added later and later the day before, the times for the second doses were different. On top of the nurses who came with the medications, another technician came a few times to take blood pressure. Anna hardly slept at all between all this and her seizures. Still, she wasn't stabilized enough for an MRI.

"We saw multiple hypermotor seizures overnight," this neurologist said. "Her movements aligned on the video. The doctors are reviewing the video EEG now."

"Was anything—" I began. I didn't know how to ask it, or even what exactly I was asking. I wanted, simply, to know if "multiple hypermotor seizures" meant anything new in all of this.

"Some seizures seemed to have a focus in the front left," she continued, without my finishing whatever I was trying to say. "But as I said, Neurology is going through the whole film now."

"Does everyone know...I'm...I'm in the hospital?" Anna said, drowsily, later that morning. "At school?"

"Well, I'm sure some know by now."

"Everybod...body...at...dance knows," she stuttered.

"Maybe," I said.

"This...sucks," she said.

"Yeah."

"Will I be...back...to...to...tonight? Dance?"

She asked that question more than a few times that day, which was much like the day before. Kristen, Geri, and I sat on either side of the bed; our frightened family and friends stopped in; Grinspan, other neurologists, pediatricians and nurses came by for updates; med doses were increased, and a heavy-eyed Anna watched television, seized, slept, and watched more television. Her dinner was a small dish of mac and cheese, with a side of carrots, a bun, and apple juice. Despite it seeming that the time between seizures was expanding slightly, the doctors couldn't say if it was the meds or that it was simply Anna being here in a hospital setting, exerting almost no energy on her body and brain. The plan was now to put her under sedation the next morning to keep her still for the MRI. I slept over again, watching the lines spike and dip to the sounds of the nature scenes channel.

In the morning of what would be our third day in the PICU, Kristen called just as Anna had been woken by the station nurse, who administered another round of meds. Kristen told me that she and Geri were outside and about to park the car with the hospital valet. She told me she'd dropped Nora off at Freddy and Samantha's, who would take her with Juliet to school.

The plan was now, we were told, to follow the MRI with an immediate PET/CT scan. This meant that yet another substance, this time radioactive, would be entered into Anna's body. The PET scan, or Positive Emission Tomography, gets three-dimensional images and is often used for cancer patients to more precisely locate tumors. The hope was to get Anna both of these procedures done while the sedation lasted.

Anna hadn't eaten since dinner, and I couldn't really remember how long it had been since I had. My head was pounding, and since Geri and Kristen had arrived, I took the opportunity to shower and change in the family facility just off the waiting lounge. I thought I'd head down to the street and get breakfast. I made the mistake of sharing this with Anna.

"So you...you get to have a nice meal," she said, scornfully.

"Yeah, but I don't think I'll enjoy it much," I said. "I'll be right back."

"No, enjoy it! Enjoy it! Take a...take a nice...nice...walk too! My legs can't move!" Her face was hot red. Kristen said nothing, stroking Anna's arm while holding her cheek against her forehead. "I want two huge cheeseburgers. And...fries!"

"Did you tell Anna the good news, Mommy?" Geri said, looking at Kristen. I couldn't imagine what good news there was. Kristen shook her head.

"You tell her, Grandma," she said.

"Well, Dr. Grinspan said no more gluten-free diet. You can eat whatever you want!"

"Oh," Anna gasped. Then: "Fuck yes."

"Anna," I said, somehow having it in me to be fed up with the cursing. "What is it with the mouth?"

"Sorry," she said snidely.

"It's been enough now," I said. "You can't talk like this no matter what."

"Sorry!"

A young man who looked about thirty walked in, wearing brown scrubs.

"Anna?" he asked. I read his identification pinned to his shirt. Anesthesiology.

"Yes, sir!" she said, perked up. I had a brief fear she'd curse at him.

He introduced himself and asked us all few questions about when Anna last ate, allergies, and whatever else. He said he'd return in a while and walked back into the hall.

"Whew! That guy is hot," Anna said.

Geri and Kristen laughed. I'd never heard her say something like that. I shook my head, which reminded me of how badly it hurt.

There was a deli near the parking garage where I'd left my car. As I walked there, I called my old friend Rich, now an ER doctor in Florida. Rich and I went to both high school and college together. I hadn't talked to him in a good year, but he'd always remained a close friend. I wanted to let him know the latest about Anna and ask his opinion on it all. This was unfair of me, as how the hell would he know anything, not being anywhere near, but I'd done this to Dr. Richard Petrik many times over the years over some medical drama big or small. He always gave me his best effort, which never failed to be a clear, reassuring breakdown of the possibilities as he could see them, based on whatever I was describing. It might have been, "Sounds like a flu, rest and stay hydrated," or "I don't think she's pregnant," or "If it still hurts Monday, get it checked out, but I doubt it's broken," and it always put me at ease.

I trusted his sense of things, even when he was guessing. From the time I'd met him in ninth grade, he always told the truth, and, like me, he was an athlete in college (football) who discovered what he wanted to be (a doctor) later than most (senior year). A difference was, Rich actually not only became it, but was a huge success. He worked at a hospital, and was head of his department.

When we'd first brought Anna to NewYork-Presbyterian, when she was a baby, Rich was doing his residency, straight out of medical school. It felt like a crazy coincidence at the time. He wasn't in pediatrics, but he still managed to gather inside information about what the doctors were thinking as we waited for answers. When he was on the night shift, he'd make his way to the PICU and review with us all he'd found out, showing us scans and explaining what they might mean. It was Rich who most thoroughly explained what a brain lesion was after we'd been told that was what Anna had. I remembered those scenes clearly now, as my call went to his voicemail somewhere in Gainesville.

I didn't leave any details in my voice message, but I asked him to call me when he could. When I got back to the PICU with my food in a plastic bag, Anna was gone. Kristen and Geri sat silently.

"They took her right after you left," Kristen said.

I saw visions of Anna terrified, being rolled out, kicking and screaming. I couldn't believe I wasn't there to help her.

"Was she okay?"

"Sure," Kristen said. "It was the same guy in the brown scrubs. Anna asked him out."

"Asked him out?"

"She had the whole place cracking up," Geri said. "We walked with them to the elevators, and she wouldn't let up. The poor man was blushing."

She and Kristen were laughing. I turned and looked at the nurse standing at the station. She was smiling wide, like she'd just seen the whole hilarious thing.

"One of the neurologists who was with them asked if this was unusual behavior for Anna," Kristen said.

"It definitely is!" I said. "I hope you said so!"

"She asked if we'd noticed any other 'disinhibition,' she called it."

"Obviously we have," I said. "She's been cursing like crazy."

"They said it can be a symptom of frontal lobe epilepsy," Geri said. "Loss of impulse control. Outbursts, anger, profanity...."

"Fair to say, we've seen it," I said.

When Anna was rolled back a few hours later, she wasn't the groggy, beaten, post-medically sedated patient I expected. The stuttering was gone. The same handsome anesthesiologist was behind her, pushing. She was sitting up, talking loudly. A nurse and the floor pediatrician were alongside, laughing.

"So what's her name?" Anna called, cocking her head back to look at him. "Your fiancée?"

"Ellen," he answered, stifling his own laughter.

Anna folded her arms, pouting, as if Ellen was the long-time rival who'd finally won.

"Boring. But so is 'Anna,'" she quipped.

The nurse walked over, smiling still. Another nurse entered the room, looking the same. It was as if the whole floor was enjoying the arrival of a celebrity comic in the house for some trifling injury.

"What does she do, this Ellen?" Anna continued.

"Anna..." I began, feeling like I should end this.

"She's a doctor."

"Well, *that* must be bad for you!" she cried, snarkily. "All day here with doctors, then you go on dates with another one?"

Another guffaw from the crowd. They'd gotten Anna to her corner now and begun reattaching the wires and machines.

"We did the MRI," the pediatrician said, as if addressing all of us. "We got some of the PET scan, but she had a seizure just as it started."

The corner may have gone silent with that, had Anna not gone on.

"Got a picture?" she said.

"Yes," said the anesthesiologist.

"Well, let's have a look," she said.

He reached for his wallet. A nurse took Anna's left hand to reinsert the IV. He handed the picture into her right.

"Wow," Anna said.

Her smirk softening, she looked intensely at the picture. Her eyes swept over the image, up, down, and across. She stared long and still, with a weak yet somehow happy smile.

"She's pretty."

"Thank you," the man said, tenderly.

"Look at her," Anna said. The wild in her tone was gone. It was as if she was looking at something that amazed her. "She's sitting on a horse. She's looks so...healthy."

I turned my head away and headed for the hall. As I got there and turned toward the doors of the PICU, I heard Anna behind me as she handed the picture back.

"If you break up with her, call me!"

The room roared one last time.

I wiped my eyes as the double doors clicked and slowly spread open. I walked toward the waiting lounge. If it's empty, I thought to myself, I'll sit there and cry until I can't anymore. That would feel good, I thought. Then I saw Grinspan, who saw me too.

"We got the MRI," he said.

"I heard about the PET," I said. "I just saw her."

"She was postictal for most of the PET, so it's fuzzy, but we see enough. It's there. It's not easy to see. You need to know where to look for it, which we do from her first scans. We can see it."

"A lesion?"

"It's obscure, but we see it."

"Okay," I said.

"I'll be presenting the case on Tuesday to the team," Grinspan continued. "We have a meeting where we look at a surgical plan and play Devil's advocate, poking holes in it. If the rest of us can refute each argument, she could be a surgical case."

Right then, I did the complete reversal from being terrified she would be a candidate for surgery to being terrified that she wouldn't be.

A woman in a business suit came around a corner toward the PICU. She walked at a quick clip. Grinspan turned, and when he saw her, had a kind of excitement in his voice.

"Dr. Hoffman," he said.

"Hi," she said, looking at me.

"So, this is premature...but just to put a face to the name...."

Then he looked at me.

"This is Mr. Palmieri, the father. I was mentioning..."

"Caitlin Hoffman," she said, putting her hand out. She looked even younger than him.

"Dr. Hoffman is our head pediatric neurosurgeon," Grinspan said, just as I took her hand in mine. "So the MRI confirms the lesion. Not to get ahead of things..."

"We meet Tuesday?" Dr. Hoffman said to him, as if enough had been said.

"Yes," Grinspan said. Hoffman turned to me again and put her hand out. We shook a second time.

"Nice to meet you, Doctor," I said. I looked at her fingers.

"Nice to meet you," she said, and walked on.

"Brain surgery," Rich said. "That's a big deal, Marc."

He had called almost instantly after Dr. Hoffman departed. Before I made it outside and walked to the corner of 68th Street and First Avenue to call him back, Grinspan stood with me in the hall and explained how his team of researchers, specialists, neurologists, and surgeons worked on cases together; how much he admired the particular interdisciplinary approach they took. There was a kind of delight in his expression, a pride, as if he wanted me to know that we'd somehow landed in the arms of the best. It wasn't salesmanship, though. It was something else.

"It's enthusiasm," Rich said. "And honestly, from what you're describing, it's at a level that's rare in medicine."

"He looked like he knew something, something incredible, if only he could, like, show me."

"He probably looked like a doctor looks when he thinks he can help someone," he said. "Someone like Anna."

"What do we do?" I said.

"Ah, I can't tell you that, man," he sighed. "But if you get this feeling, this kind of feeling for this doctor, it sounds like you should keep listening."

"This is horrible," I said. "All of it. I can't believe it's come to this. Her whole life, it's like one of us was standing right next to her, waiting for some pill to finally work. And if one never did, we'd be happy just to stay there, next to her. We'd do anything. Anything but this. Brain surgery. Oh my god."

"I can't imagine."

"I want someone to take over for me, Rich," I said. "Take the wheel. It's like you and I are headed back to Carolina from home after break. I got us as far as the border of Virginia, but I'm done. Your turn. Wake me up in Winston-Salem. Is that how we did it?"

"Ah...I miss that."

"I miss everything," I said.

We were silent a moment.

"Caitlin Hoffman," Rich said. "I'm looking at her bio now. She's big time. And as a woman, to get where she is in this business, it means she's even bigger."

"I looked at her hands," I said. "I wanted to look at them, and look hard, because they could be the hands that go into her brain. Those hands...."

"Yeah," he said.

I looked down 68th street. The cars, the traffic lights, the sliver of western sky.

"Marc. Listen," Rich said. "This I can tell you. From what you're telling me about this doctor, what he says about his department...is that he wants a shot. It sounds like he thinks they can do it, and if they all agree, and it sounds like they will...that's all I can say. I can say...he really wants a shot."

I told him I'd keep him posted. I put the phone in my pocket, turned around, set my eyes east, and headed back to the hospital.

CHAPTER ELEVEN

"WILL I DIE?"

"**G**ood afternoon, all. We have a special visitor today here to talk to us about his career. He committed himself a long time ago to his dream—to someday succeed in the theatre— as an actor, a writer...on Broadway, then in Hollywood movies, and network television."

"I love you in *Shades of Blue*!" called out one of the students from the middle of the lecture hall.

"As some of you clearly know, my friend here has just finished two seasons on NBC's *Shades of Blue* starring alongside Jennifer Lopez."

Applause.

"You'll get a chance to ask all the questions you want before each group performs your scene for his feedback. I introduce to you my old, dear friend, and long-ago roommate, Michael Laurence."

The students applauded again. Michael humbly waved as he approached to sit on the lip of the lecture hall stage, to take my place, as I moved to the first row to take a seat.

"Thank you, Marc. It's so cool to be here and meet you all!"

Hands flew up, and he began answering eager questions about preparing for roles, life on sets, auditions, and, of course, working with movie stars. I smiled and raised my eyebrows as I tried to listen, but most of my attention was again on my phone. Anna had been nearly stabilized for two days now by a course of dexamethasone, a steroid that the doctors hoped would temporarily reduce the inflammation of the brain lesion. She wasn't seizure free by any means, and this would only be a short-term stopgap against the clusters, but she was stable enough to be transferred from the PICU to the "step-down" floor, where Kristen had stayed with her for two nights. Anna was now on four other medications besides this steroid, all at high dosages. She was visited by a physical therapist each afternoon for rehab. She couldn't walk at first, having been in a bed for so long, having seized so much, and being so drugged.

Because Kristen had gotten the few medical emergency days off from her school, I was able to get to my final City College class and then to Dobbs Ferry for my Wednesday Mercy classes. The semester was so close to finishing, and I was still attempting to finish things on the strongest note possible. The students had been excited about Michael's visit for weeks.

It was also the afternoon of Dr. Grinspan's surgical conference. As I sat there in the lecture hall, the class starstruck by my friend, I knew that a team of researchers, neurologists, and brain surgeons, including Dr. Nangia, Dr. Hoffman, and the neurosurgeon who knew Julie, Dr. Theodore Schwartz, were in a conference room somewhere at the hospital. They were studying Anna's case history, films of scans new and old, EEG readouts, and published case histories, trying to determine whether the risks of going into Anna's brain outweighed the possible but never-guaranteed benefits. At any moment, the verdict would be in, letting us know if she was eligible for this homerun swing or not. The class time passed with no news from Kristen.

Michael and I took a stroll around the grounds, down to the bank of the Hudson River and back toward the softball field closer to where my office was, where a game against rival Molloy College was in progress. Music played through the loudspeakers between innings as we got to his car.

"What a beautiful campus this is. Those students are great. You're lucky, man," he said.

"I know," I said, and as for having this job, I meant it. As for having Anna's condition finally asserting itself in its full brutality, maybe not so much. I could tell Michael picked up on this duality a fast as I did.

"Anna's going to pull out of this," he said.

"Yeah," I said. "Well, it can't stay the way it is. For better or worse."

He took a deep breath and leaned back on his car, looking around at the scenery, the softball crowd, the lush grass field behind us, the dorms in the distance, the river…. I knew what he was trying to do. And I'd seen others try the same: to find a way to transition out of the subject at hand, for both our sakes.

"This is gonna be a great life here, working here. And I can totally see Anna and Nora, meeting you right here after class, by the softball field, for a dinner with their dad at the 'caf.'"

He'd known me so long that I knew that he knew I'd dreamed of that future moment from the second I got this job. I smiled, and maybe I said something of a thank you as he got in his car—but I didn't say much. I knew I didn't have to.

It wasn't quite an hour later when the phone rang. The noise startled me as I drove. I was so tired that on my brisk, trafficless ride on the Hutchinson Parkway, I had achieved a sort of waking sleep. Seeing it was Kristen's number, I knew the wait was up. She would have spoken to the team and learned their decision.

"They just came to our room," she said. "Anna's a candidate for surgery."

"What did they say?"

"Very specific details about the lesion."

"Like what?"

"It turns out it's considered pretty big. They said it's cone-shaped, and it runs from near the surface all the way, or almost all the way, to something called...."

I heard the sound of her legal pad pages flipping fast and furious.

"The basal ganglia," she continued. "And it has been there all her life, since birth."

"All those years, it's that big, and all those scans couldn't see it?"

"They said it happens. It's nobody's fault. It isn't easy to see."

"All that time, we're thinking it was something that was disappearing. Now, I can't believe what I'm hearing. But, of course, I *can* believe it. Because it's awful."

"The surgeons will be Hoffman and Schwartz," she continued. "Dr. Hoffman will be the lead surgeon."

"You mean *would* be," I said, defensively. I felt like Kristen had just taken a decisive leap I wasn't ready for. "Let's slow down a second. Okay? What does all this mean? The surgery...then what? What do they think?"

"They think it's worth trying."

"Wait. Wait. *Trying?*"

"That's a good thing," she said.

"Is it?" I said. "Slow down a second. Obviously, we need to talk about this. Get a second opinion."

"Marc—"

"You've told me almost nothing here. What area of the brain would be affected? Injured? What's left of her after this?" I started yelling. "We can't do this! Kristen, we cannot do this!"

"The surgery would be considered a major surgery."

"Yeah, no shit! How are you not screaming right now?"

"I don't know," she said, her voice finally cracking. I guess I got what I wanted. To hear her hurting just as I was.

"Fuck this," I said, gripping the steering wheel. I might have been going one hundred. "We gotta find another way. Get a second opinion."

"They say she has about a seventy percent chance," Kristen went on.

"That number again. It's always seventy percent. Seventy percent that meds will work, seventy percent it will go away on its own, seventy percent this, that, whatever."

"I'm looking at her right now, Marc," she said. "At this point, I'd take the bet on a lot worse odds."

She still sounded calm, too calm, like we weren't talking about what surgeons said about our child but about what some plumber said was an estimate for something that needed fixing in the house.

"So what do they mean by that this time? Seventy percent chance at what?" I said. "Making it through alive?"

Suddenly the sight of Anna's arm, heavy and immobile that morning in Todd's Paralysis, came into mind. Dead looking. A limb, hanging there, at her side, dead.

"And what's the thirty percent, then? Thirty percent she ends up what? Worse than she is now? Paralyzed?"

Silence. A sniffle.

"I can't...I can't...." she stammered. Then, as if in a breakdown: "Oh my God."

"Okay. Kristen," I said, softer, now regretting that I broke her. "Nothing is in stone. We can talk, we will research, we can find another opinion. Nothing is for sure. Nobody seems to have ever known what this is, and we have to keep our heads."

After a moment of saying nothing, her voice was back.

"They think they can discharge her from here in a few days. We would have a meeting with the doctors right after discharge to ask any questions. Then we can take her home until the surgery."

"Okay. Okay. Just...."

"I'm going to hang up now," Kristen said. "I've been crying and I'm exhausted. I just want to lie down and hold her. Okay?"

"One last question."

I was approaching the Throgs Neck Bridge.

"Did they say...for the surgery...is it like...something they want to do, soon?"

"Weeks. Not months. She's in a lot of danger."

*

We were discharged on a Thursday, the ninth day of Anna's hospital stay. As explained to Kristen after the surgical conference, our first follow-up would be immediate, as fast as we could get to Weill Cornell's Multidisciplinary Neurology/Neurosurgery Clinic about a city block north.

While we awaited the discharge papers, we packed our things, including the many well-wish cards and gift baskets Anna had received from family and friends, as well as our work colleagues and my baseball parents. The steroid had continued to lessen the seizure frequency and intensity, and with the physical therapy, she was now able to walk, if slowly, and leaning on one of us. The stream of her visitors had helped Anna regain some strength, too, friends and family often holding her up by the arms as she insisted on attempting short walks in the hall. After Annmarie had come from the studio for a second visit, Anna was so happy that she attempted something of a pirouette and nearly crashed to the floor, tangled in mobile EEG wiring.

The discharge paperwork listed the procedures she had undergone since we'd arrived: video EEG, brain MRI, and brain PET/CT scan. The imaging summaries all read "cortical dysplasia," just as Dr. Merchant called it when Anna was an infant in this same hospital. The papers also listed the four antiseizure medications she would stay on.

Our meeting took place in a small examination room. Present were Dr. Hoffman, Dr. Nangia, Physician Assistant Jackie LaMothe, and others. We discussed the plan to slightly reduce two of the medications over the following weeks, as Anna was on too many, and the doses were too high, to not risk toxicity and liver damage. Dr. Nangia and Jackie composed a plan for a four-week partial dose reduction for the Lacosamide and Levetiracetam, in the hopes that we would see a relief of Anna's agitated and giddy behavior. These two meds would each be lowered incrementally until surgery. Once this plan was set down on paper, the orders were sent by computer to a pharmacy near our home in Queens. Docusate, for constipation that all the medication caused, Vitamin B6, and a new rescue med pack were also ordered, as well as a pill form of the Valium, to be used when seizure clusters emerged, most expected in the evenings.

Dr. Nangia reexplained, once and for all, the cause of Anna's epilepsy. The lesion was scarred brain tissue that disrupted neurons and leaked electricity until the brain's entire network went afire. Dr. Hoffman explained the plan: a craniotomy, corticectomy, and lesionectomy. The lesion would be located with the greatest precision they could arrive at by coordinating the readings of multiple kinds of scans, then cut out. A scan she had yet to undergo, something called a magnetoencephalography, or MEG scan, done by a machine that only existed at a handful of American hospitals, would be necessary to help best home in on the surgical target. It shook me that in this type of surgery, no actual visible difference between the lesion and healthy brain tissue could be detected by the naked eye of the surgeons—it was all pinpointed by overlapping scan readings, like planes in a fog relying on radar and the flight tower. Where all the scans pinpointed the epileptic activity would be the location resected.

I pushed for details. And I got them, for better and worse. The top area of the skull just above her forehead would be crushed, then parted, so the surgeons could access the lesion. Afterward, the bones would be reconstructed, held in place by titanium plates; fastened by screws. A scar would run from one side of her head at about ear level up and over to about the same spot on the opposite side.

We were given a copy of a medical research paper on a recent study of ten pediatric patients who underwent a similar procedure for brain lesions, though in varying locations in the brain. The outcomes were broken down into classes of improvement or non-improvement: "Seizure free," "Almost seizure free," "Worthwhile improvement," and "No worthwhile improvement." Two of the ten had no improvement. One had some, and seven were now seizure free. This was the seventy percent they mentioned. It looked promising, in the context we were in, until we looked closer at the four patients who had the most similar lesion location to Anna's. Those outcomes were evenly distributed across all four recorded outcomes, from best to worst.

Kristen and I hadn't yet had a chance to talk about it extensively, but we tacitly agreed to get a second opinion about all this. Either way, one thing had become more than obvious. Life attempting to treat Anna with only medication was untenable now. For this reason, when it came time for our questions, we found ourselves asking far more about the "how" than the "why." Meanwhile, Anna lay still on the bed, sporadically mumbling voices at the wall, quietly clownish, regardless of who may see or hear. I didn't think she was listening to anything we were saying, which I didn't mind, considering what was being described. I was wrong.

"Will they cut my hair off?" Anna blurted out. She remained facing the wall, grinning. "Will they shave it bald?"

The answer was a quick "no" from Dr. Hoffman. No, not at all, and in fact, she explained, the healed scar would be nicely buried beneath that long hair of hers and eventually no thicker than a pencil line.

"Okay," Anna said. "I have another question. Will I die?"

I jerked toward her in my stool, as if she'd said something inappropriate. But I quickly realized this was the question I myself wanted to ask, probably most of all, but wouldn't ever have.

"No," Dr. Hoffman said, unflinching.

Anna said nothing.

Of course, I found this categorical answer unconvincing. The general anesthesia given for her MRIs in the past always came with some small risk she would never wake up. I knew this, we all knew this, and now here we were not only going under general anesthesia, but we were one errant flick of the blade away from who knows what. Trying not to sound doubting of Dr. Hoffman's confidence, I followed with questions about arteries and vessels or whatever other precious channels were vulnerable.

"Is the lesion close to anything sensitive?" I said, instantly feeling like a fool. How could anything in the brain not be near anything sensitive? The whole thing is sensitive.

"In our business, a millimeter is a football field," Hoffman said.

"So then," I said, trying to accept some assurance, "what are the...things that..." I didn't know how to finish, not with Anna right there, who clearly was listening.

"The things that would put her back in the operating room would be bleeding at the site," Hoffman started.

"Right," I said.

"Or an infection," she continued. "Those are always things we watch for. She would be monitored in the PICU and by scans post-surgically. If we see something, we go back in."

"How bad could...."

"Could that get," she was finishing for me now, nodding, like she was completing a sentence, not a question, like she had these conversations every day. "We are confident that any damage would be something Anna would eventually recover from."

"Eventually," I said, weakly.

"We do not expect that problem," Hoffman resumed. There wasn't a hint of insecurity in her voice. It felt she almost wanted to say, "If I could tell you this is your only option, I would. But I don't want to say it like that, so I'm trying to make you see it."

Rich once told me that neurosurgeons were different animals than neurologists. The latter lived in a mysterious mangle of synapses and shadowy, unknown regions of brain nobody could predict anything about, phenomena that humanity is only beginning to observe and attempt to understand. Neurosurgeons were mechanics who saw the brain more like an engine, where a thing might need adjustment or replacement here and there, before they close the hood, start it back up, and send it on its way.

"The location of the lesion," Dr. Nangia said, "isn't near movement, speech, or balance."

"Where is it located?" Kristen asked.

"Executive function," Nangia replied.

Hoffman jumped back in quickly.

"The limits to what we can remove will be determined by what Anna is and isn't using. We are removing useless tissue. Nothing she uses. And the MEG scan she'll have will help us know more."

This brought us back to the MEG machine, the closest one being located at Overlook Hospital in Summit, New Jersey, where they had already begun arranging for our appointment. We then discussed the series of other pre-operative appointments that would be necessary, like a pediatrician's presurgical clearance, a neuropsych exam, and blood tests. The surgery was already on the books, scheduled for just over a month out, as Drs. Hoffman and Schwartz wanted to convene their specific team of specialists in the operating room that day, from the nurses, radiologists, and surgical assistants to the reconstructive surgeons.

"We don't want to wait, for obvious reasons," Hoffman said. "This is about the soonest we can do it, coordinating everyone's availability."

Until then, we understood, this was a matter of keeping her alive long enough to get her into that operating room. That is, if we agreed to do it, if some second opinion we had no idea yet where to get failed to somehow give us hope in some other way.

On the way to the elevator, I checked the time. I was surprised. It was far earlier in the day than it felt like. We would even most likely beat the rush hour traffic on the FDR to the bridge. I decided that after we'd picked Nora up from Freddy and Samantha's, gotten the prescriptions, unpacked the car, and got things settled at the house, I'd head out to my evening baseball practice at the indoor facility Next Level used on Long Island.

The thought of me being there, throwing baseballs for batting practice or hitting groundballs to our infielders, somehow made room for a deeper breath than I'd taken for many hours.

"Anna?" a young man's soft voice called out toward us as we stood at the elevator bank.

We looked back toward the department waiting area and saw a medical student we'd met during our stay who was in training, shadowing many of the doctors most of the days we were in the PICU and the step-down floor. He had given Anna her many neuro examinations as she lay in her bed, the kind where she'd be asked to hold out her arms, then touch her nose, or push back with resistance on his open hand, etc. He had always been a calm presence in all the hubbub of the coming and going of everyone else. He walked our way.

"I'm so glad to hear you're going home now," he said.

"Same here, I think," I said.

"We don't know what to do," Kristen said. "They are saying surgery in a month. I'm terrified."

He looked at Kristen with a small, sympathetic smile. Then, he turned to Anna, who was standing beside me.

"Look, Anna," he said, reaching into his lab coat pocket. "I keep this with me."

He revealed a half sheet of paper, on which was drawn a colored flower, the kind that Anna had begun drawing off the lessons on YouTube. I hadn't noticed her doing that in the hospital.

"Did Anna draw that?" Kristen asked.

"She did," he said. I looked down at Anna. She stared down, weary, and as if she hadn't heard him. "And she gave it to me."

He moved toward Anna, crouched down, and his face was at the level of hers.

"Oh, hi," she said.

"Hi, Anna," he said.

She looked up, then hugged him.

"Goodbye. I'll miss seeing you. But I know you're going to do great and have a very happy life."

"Thank you," she said. He put his open hand on her cheek.

The elevator doors opened.

"Take care," I said. "Thank you."

Anna followed me in. Kristen took a step toward the elevator doors but stopped suddenly, turning back to the medical student.

"If this was your child," she said, firmly, but trembling. "What would you do? Honestly. The surgery. Would you do it?"

The young man, unfazed, slowly placed Anna's drawing back in his pocket.

"I'd do it," he said.

The doors closed between us. The elevator descended. Kristen stared ahead. So did I. I knew. She did too. We'd just gotten our second opinion.

For a decade, we used a pediatric pharmacy on East 66th Street in Manhattan called Cherry's. It had an area where kids could sit and play with toys, read books, and even a small electric train that ran the store perimeter on tracks mounted overhead. They had a specialty of sweetening up kids' medicines to taste yummy—like candy—theoretically making it easier on parents to administer to small children.

Cherry's was near NewYork-Presbyterian, and we filled our very first prescription there after our first discharge when Anna was five months old. As we packed our baby up to return to our Astoria apartment and suddenly-very-changed new life as parents, my father took the few-block walk to pick up the first of the many different drugs she'd be prescribed in her life ahead.

I was often in Manhattan for my different jobs, so we kept our business there all the while. I liked the owner, whom I'd ask for feedback from other patients about whatever new med we were getting, and he was always helpful, full of reliable information.

Now, with things in such flux, and knowing I wouldn't be leaving our house unless absolutely necessary until surgery, we had the prescription sent to a CVS blocks away in Bayside. It was a huge order, and I wondered, as I stood waiting for the pharmacist to fill it and tally up the co-payments, if she was wondering about the details of whatever case "Anna Palmieri" was that would require this many anticonvulsants.

I'd left Anna with Kristen, Geri, Bruce, and my parents at our house and picked Nora up on the way to CVS. She got in the back seat, waved to Juliet, then started crying almost immediately.

"I missed Anna," she said. "But I tried not to think of her."

"That's okay, honey."

"I didn't want to throw up at Juliet's."

I then gave Nora the rosiest possible report to her about Anna's outlook, but also tried to get her ready for what was waiting at home.

"Anna's not herself right now," I said. "She's on a lot of medicines, and because of that, she feels very weak and tired and out of it. Okay?"

"Yeah," Nora said.

"You're being amazing, Nora. Thank you."

"Can we get doughnuts, then?"

A box of chocolate donuts, Nora's favorite, sat beside a foot-long plastic pill organizer case to the growing group of our orange prescription bottles on the pharmacy checkout counter.

With Kristen and the grandparents now at the house, able to watch Anna and get Nora to and from tonight's dance class, and with baseball practice starting in about three hours, I found myself with a little time. I changed clothes and drove out to the indoor baseball facility we used for our nighttime workouts. I sat in the parking lot with my iPhone and wrote emails to students who still owed me work before the grade deadline and to Cohen Children's Hospital billing department, who had gone ahead and issued a $1,260.00 tab for the private room, which by now seemed like a distant memory. Despite that annoyance, when I got all that done, I actually felt, for a moment, that things were as much "under control" as they could possibly be.

"I'm heading into practice," I said to Kristen on the phone. "Everything secure?"

"Your dad's getting diner food," she said. "Want anything from the diner?"

"Big fat cheeseburger and fries, extra gluten," I said. "Where is she?"

"Asleep, on the sofa. She seemed so happy to be home, called a couple friends, but got tired."

"Please watch her close," I said.

"Everyone is."

I walked into the warehouse-sized sports facility. Country music blasted through the mounted speakers. Mixed within were the smacks of baseballs being hit in the batting tunnels and shouts of coaches giving direction. I saw Mike Ambort standing with another coach my age, Ciro Ambrosio, who was drafted by the same Toronto scout that drafted me, and before long, I felt my head relax into a kind of soothing order.

I was here, at practice, for one. That had to be a good sign. Second, there would be no more wondering about the cause of Anna's seizures. We knew what the source was and had made a plan of action. We had a date, time, and place. This clarity almost felt like stability, and now, I could set it all aside for a while and play some ball. Of course, this mindset would only stick if I prevented myself from actually dwelling on what this surgery entailed, and what life would be like if we lost Anna.

Manning usually had all the practice plans, but he wasn't coming tonight. Ambort, Ciro, and I stood some yards from the players, as they did their stretching and throwing, and planned how we'd rotate the groups through the batting, fielding, and pitching areas.

"How's your daughter?" Ciro asked. I supposed he felt he'd waited long enough for me to bring it up.

"I don't know," I said. I really wanted to give a good quick answer and take the pitchers to the bullpen tunnels. "Brain surgery in six weeks."

"Holy shit," he said. He mentioned that he had some kind of holy oil at home and wanted to make sure I wiped some on her before the operation. He was a believer and a saint of a guy.

"You should talk to my cousin," Ambort added. "I think her son had surgery. I haven't seen them in a bit."

"I'd love to."

I recalled him telling me about his cousin but not about a surgery. I thought it'd be a gift to hear whatever she had to say.

"I'll text you her number."

We practiced, and my cell didn't ring or ping once. I threw short-toss batting practice much of the evening, and reviewed pickoff moves with the pitchers on the hard rubber mounds, before overseeing the bullpens. I felt lively. The hat, sweatpants, and baseball shirt felt good to be in, the costume in which I could always slip into one of my oldest, most comforting roles.

Practice ended at eight, early enough for me to call Ambort's cousin the minute I got back in my car, plugged my phone in, and started the engine. I got Donna's voicemail and left a quick message, realizing just then that I hadn't asked Mike if he'd warned her that I might be calling.

I headed west toward the Cross Island Parkway, which runs from southern Queens to its northern edge. The Long Island air was heavy and sweet—baseball air, night game air. In my final year of baseball, at twenty-two, I'd become the pitcher on our staff at Wake Forest with the standing referred to as the "Friday starter," since the in-conference series would begin on Fridays, running through the weekends. Because I'd pitch these first games, I was often matched against whoever was the ace on the opposing team.

These were some of the best college teams in the country: Clemson, Florida State, Georgia Tech...and so the games were often excruciatingly close, with a small handful of runs in total, battled out defensively. My head coach, George Greer, who went on to become a bench coach in the big leagues with the St. Louis Cardinals, spoke consolingly to me after I lost a tight game at the University of Georgia.

"When two good pitchers face off," he said, "any threat either team puts up could mean the whole game. Any mistake anyone makes could mean the whole game. One good or bad play, one swing, one miss, one act of God, and the whole thing's won or lost. Your job is to keep us in it. That's all you can do."

The pitcher's job is pretty simple: keep the team alive, inning by inning, to stay neck and neck with the opposition, until a break comes. There are tense moments, men in scoring position, the game a mental test—but if you stay focused, keep it close, you've done your job. I graduated the second winningest pitcher in school history, so I'd gutted out enough of those edgy innings in my career, win or lose, to start seeing life the same way. Maybe it was the clothes or that fragrant air through my windows, but that night made me feel like I was at the start of something like one of those games. Here we were, the first inning of a six-week stretch to the surgery that, while certain to be grueling, was almost refreshingly as simple to me as baseball. Day to day, hour to hour, minute to minute, I had to stand by Anna, catch her when she fell, watch that she was still breathing once a seizure passed, and every twelve hours, sort, count, and deliver with utmost exactness her blue, amber, red, white, and pink pills. I had to keep her in it until she was in the surgeons' hands, and the game went whatever way it would go.

I hadn't planned on calling home, for fear of Kristen's phone ringing and stirring a sleeping Anna, but as I approached our exit, Kristen called me.

"I'm almost there," I said. "What's the scene?"

"We're just getting back," she said.

"From where?"

"Dance."

"I thought my father was bringing Nora back."

"We all went. Anna insisted."

I figured Anna wanted to see her dance friends as they exited the building. Most of them had been calling, FaceTiming, or sending cards since Anna was out. I worried she'd been put at risk of a seizure in front of all of them, of course, but just as much, I worried about her behavior, if she would be able speak coherently or not say anything wild or inappropriate.

"This wasn't smart, Kristen. We need to be safe."

"Anna insisted. She put her leotard on when she woke up."

"Wait. She *went to class?*"

"Annmarie said she watched her closely the whole time. Nora did the same. Whenever she felt anything coming on, she took a break."

"Took a break?" I said, incredulously. "From what? Stumbling around, dizzy and oblivious? She should be on the sofa, sleeping, watched closely, by you!"

"And she was. Then she woke up and asked if Nora was at dance. I said yes, and she got up and started getting dressed. I said she should stay here, but she didn't say anything except to take her to the studio."

"And you did. No argument? You just…took her like any normal day?"

"I called first. They said they wanted her to come and that they'd watch her. I waited in the lobby. Anna wouldn't take no for an answer."

"You're the parent, Kristen. You tell the child what's what. Not the other way around."

"She wanted to go, Marc. Annmarie told me she even did a dance she said she made up in the hospital."

"I can't believe what I'm hearing. She cannot go! She's in grave goddamn danger! A 'close eye' on her doesn't help when she goes into a massive seizure, drops, and smashes her head on a studio floor! The lesion is bad enough, but let's avoid adding a concussion on top of it!"

"The recital is in two weeks. She wants to rehearse."

"The recital? She can't walk straight! Kristen, the kid can collapse at any moment, every moment. She's not going on a stage for a fucking show!"

Kristen was silent. My mind and emotions were brawling. And I was speeding again.

"Obviously," I said, "this year, there is no recital for Anna. We're not going to let our kid go out there in front of four hundred happy, unsuspecting people and give them the shocking spectacle of their lives. No way."

"We'll talk when you get home."

Seventy now. Eighty, up the Cross Island.

"She's shutting it down, all of it," I went on, through gritted teeth. "She hasn't gone a day without seizures since April, and you let her go there tonight? And suggest she participate in a recital? She's disabled, Kristen. Let's hope she's still alive this summer. Until then, she's sitting it out. All of it."

Kristen hung up.

CHAPTER TWELVE

SHOWDOWN

I n the morning, I would see Nora off on her walk to school, then make sure Anna swallowed her pills. The morning dose included five. At night, it was the same, not including the Valium. She was having significant seizures overnight, but in the daytime, she'd remain in a kind of stupor, lying on the sofa watching television, unsettled now and then by shakes that drained away after a few flicks of the eyelids and upper body trembles.

I did my best not to leave the living room or kitchen, where I could keep at least half an eye and ear on Anna. Most of that time, I spent with my laptop, tackling the last of finalizing grades, filling out the end of year summaries, answering emails from students begging for a little more time on that last assignment, and arranging the preoperative medical appointments we needed to get done. I was also making calls to the New York City Department of Education and Anna's middle school for them to assign a visiting teacher to begin at-home schooling so that she would meet her attendance requirement for sixth grade. It was clear that she was in no state to learn much, but at this point in the school year, an excess of absences was the only threat to her not being promoted.

When Nora returned from school, I'd make sure both girls changed into their leotards, packed their bags with the jazz, tap, and ballet shoes, and drive them to the studio. Anna still insisted on attending class, and I'd quit arguing. As one would expect, she never got very far into any of them without having to leave. I'd drop the girls off, park the car, sit in the lobby, and at around forty minutes in, I'd get the text, usually from Nora, that Anna had removed herself from the group and sat down or staggered out into the hall. I'd go to the studio room they were in, walk her outside and back out to the car. Her face would be inflamed, and she'd be crying, describing that she couldn't breathe, or felt her knees lock, or how there was no feeling in her feet.

My surrender on the dance issue was based on a compromise with Kristen. I wouldn't complain about Anna attending these last classes of the year, and Kristen would agree that the dance recital was out of the question. I believed I'd thought of a way I hoped would satisfy Anna's desire to finish her dance year with some sort of performance, without actually being in front of an audience: letting her do the dress rehearsal. Since it was my idea, and I seemed so pleased with it, Kristen told me I'd be the one to inform Anna.

To make it as clear and inviting as I could, I came up with a personal analogy to illustrate how I sympathized with how hard it was to sit on the sidelines with an injury. In my Oral Communications courses, we call this strategy "establishing ethos," a credibility. The speaker gives an example of how he himself walked the walk, and so the listener should trust him when he talks the talk.

"You're a teammate, just like I was," I told her. It was morning; Anna was under a blanket on the sofa, staring ahead at the television. *The Greatest Showman*, yet again. "A dancer is part of a team, a group of performers who practice together, just like a baseball team. The goal for both groups is similar. Right? To perform together when it's game time. Or showtime!"

Her eyes widened as I spoke, then blinked in rapid succession. Her hands gripped her blanket as if she was suddenly going over a waterfall, and the blanket was a life preserver. As fast as the seizure began, it was gone, and Anna was back watching the movie like nothing happened. The night prior, she'd had four, one time nearly throwing herself off the bed and onto me, on the floor.

"There's no shame in missing this one," I went on. "I had to do it once. Sophomore year. It was an entire fall practice season, which is really important in college. I'd hurt my shoulder pitching in my summer season and had to rest it. That was the only way to get healthy again and get back out there. I had to sit in the dugout while the rest of the team practiced, so I could be ready for the games in the spring."

Even then, I felt a touch of regret. My shoulder really was never the same, and I was never sure if it was the tendonitis I had, or the fact that I went nearly an entire offseason without throwing. I had also long wondered if it ultimately was the reason I wasn't drafted again my senior year. Sometimes, when professional scouts think an arm is vulnerable to injury, they take a pass on a prospect, even if he'd been drafted before and was throwing at average Major League speed.

"It was frustrating," I said. "But I knew I'd be back, and I knew I'd be glad I let myself heal first."

Anna kept her eyes on the movie like I wasn't there. Handsome Hugh Jackman was singing the blues again because his circus had burned down. The dream was dead, it seemed, but no! A moment later, the even more handsome Zac Efron announces he will pay for a new one, and everyone is singing.

Everything I was saying to Anna made great sense to myself. I was buoyed by a confidence that she'd come to see things my way, and even feel a certain dignity and maturity, some *esprit de corps*, to sit in the wings on recital day in sacrificial professionalism, just as her dad had once done in baseball.

The dress rehearsal was scheduled for a few days before the recital at the venue, and since there was no audience allowed in the seats other than one parent per dancer, mostly moms, I felt Anna could be on stage for however long she could keep on her feet. If something went wrong, Kristen would be there to grab her. If Anna got through one number, I thought, just one, at least she'd have gotten that far, enough to feel she'd completed something of what she worked all year for. As a playwright, I knew well how final dresses could feel just as exciting as an opening night, and every bit as much as an accomplishment, despite the empty seats, save whatever invited friends or family were in the back rows. It would bring a closure, I thought. I told her all that too.

*

Mercy College's 83rd Commencement Exercises would take place on Wednesday, May 16, one day before the girls' dress rehearsal, at the Westchester County Center in White Plains. It was about two hours from Bayside, and it would be the final day we'd need Geri to cover for me. After these few morning hours were done, I could be with Anna all day, every day until the surgery, leaving only for my baseball work after Kristen returned from her school on Long Island.

I was wearing my Rockport shoes, khakis, a reasonably new oxford shirt, and a twenty-year-old tie. My rented master's gown was still in its plastic wrap in the Corolla's back seat. The only commencements I'd ever been to were as a graduating student: first at Wake Forest, then City College. This was my very first as faculty, since adjuncts didn't get a seat on the stage. I'd be up there in the gown, cap, tassel, and hood. I might otherwise have been a little nervous, were I not entirely focused on getting right back to the house. I hoped to be home before the girls were ready to go to dance class.

However much I was looking toward my exit, the personal significance of the event itself didn't elude me. I had officially completed my first year at Mercy. Despite all that was going down at home, I'd managed to miss almost no class time or meetings, I'd gotten the theatre club show done, my students seemed satisfied with my courses, and I had been given a happy classroom peer observation. As I drove up the Hutchinson Parkway, I thought with irony how the Corolla key stuck in the ignition just above my right knee still shared its ring with a number of others—not only my office at Mercy, but those from jobs past—the high school gym, the periodontists' office, the insurance office, even some of the former apartments I'd lived in. I thought to myself how absurd it was that I still kept them and that I ought to hold my own little ceremony later that day, maybe as I sat in the studio lobby waiting for the alert on Anna, by throwing the old keys in the garbage.

My phone rang. I felt the usual jolt, fearing it was a 911 from home, but it wasn't. I saw it was a number I didn't recognize, with a Long Island area code.

"Is this Marc?" a woman said.

"Yes."

"Hi. It's Donna. Michael Ambort's cousin."

I'd found that only with other parents of children with epilepsy could I comfortably share the full, detailed extent of Anna's condition, and our life around it. Normally, when asked about how she was doing, I would downplay the negative as best I could, and emphasize the relative positive. Rather than go into what her seizures were like, or how many she'd had lately, or the general depression that came with thoughts of what her future would be, I would answer with how well she was doing socially, or how grateful we were that her seizures were only nocturnal so that she could continue to live her daily life—which was oh so happily full with school, Girl Scouts, sports…dance. I would say, perhaps, "Hoping she outgrows it!" Then, I'd quickly ask how their kids were doing.

I rarely had the stomach to be honest. It would feel almost cruel. In the same way most of us never really answer the casual question "How are you?" when bumping into an acquaintance, I would answer questions about Anna. Telling the full truth would call for a response on the spot that expressed not only upset and sympathy, but some kind of forced optimism. Why bring people that far down, I figured, especially when they were only being polite and loving in asking about my daughter.

With Donna, though, like the others we'd met along the way, there was no such filtering. She'd lived it all, was still living it, and we almost instantly got to comparing notes, after she told me that her cousin had given her a general idea about Anna and that she'd been praying for her since.

"Adolescence seems to be when things can go really haywire," she said.

"Right," I said. "As if their childhoods were so neat and easy."

She laughed. That's another thing about talking with fellow parents of epileptics. We could find we were able to laugh even as we shook our heads, in bleak awe of what we'd had to do to keep our children alive.

We covered the usual ground: the different meds we'd tried, side effects, how long they worked, if at all, the sleeping arrangements, the battles with school districts for proper accommodations, the wear and tear of living in watchfulness, the fear of what they'd someday do to make a living, or just live, when we were no longer around to help them.

"Mine is in his twenties," Donna said. "Right now, the issue is, he wants a car."

I laughed this time. It's about as normal as normal gets for a young person to want a car, and to hear that bit of normal, anything normal, could exist for her son, and maybe someday in Anna's twenties too, filled me with an intense, if passing joy, so intense that I laughed.

She said that they'd lately been trying the hemp cannabis treatment, and I gave her Dr. Chin's information. Her son's had been a difficult case, much like Anna's. They never successfully managed his seizures with medication. This point led me to bringing up the surgery. When I told her we were going that direction and that I'd understood they had been through it, there came a silence that hadn't yet been there in our conversation. Then, she took a deep breath.

"Michael told me. Yes. It sounds like you are in very good hands."

"Well, I can't imagine, cannot picture, actually going through with it. Can't picture actually sitting there in some waiting area, while she's in the operating…"

She cut me off.

"Every case is so different…I'm…I'm sure they're very confident it's the right thing."

"When Mike mentioned your son, I—"

"Marc."

She stopped me again, stifling a cry. Something was wrong. "Yes."

"I've been struggling with this since you called me."

"Okay. It's okay...."

"I've been praying for Anna," she said again.

"I know," I said, starting to cry too. It was something in her voice. "Thank you for that."

"Every case is different. I want you to know—"

"Of course. I do."

"But I am compelled. I am compelled to tell you...I have to."

"Anything, Donna. Please. Thank you."

"My son. During his surgery. He stroked on the table."

I immediately expressed how sorry I was to hear this, how thankful to her that she told me, that this was precisely why I called her and that I was so sorry, so sorry.

And she immediately repeated how Anna's case is surely different, that even in the few years since her son's procedure, no doubt so much more has been learned about brain surgery, how everything advances so much, so quickly. She added that while the rehabilitation was long, her son had made progress, so much they felt he was possibly fully recovered from any damage left by the stroke.

"I believe they will help her," she said. "I truly do."

I was rolling into a parking spot at the Westchester County Center. It had taken me a few laps in the lot to find one. Students in blowing blue gowns passed, parents taking cell phone videos passed, faculty I recognized passed. One waved to me.

Donna and I said our goodbyes. I thanked her for her prayers, for calling me back, for her honesty, and her example. It was hard to hang up.

I knew by now that we had no alternative. Anna was worsening every day, and even too many medications couldn't stop the seizures. What Donna had told me was no surprise, really. I knew what we were facing and what could happen. I hadn't been totally honest with Donna, I realized, when I said I couldn't imagine myself on the day of the surgery, in a waiting room, or wherever, with Anna on the table, as she put it. I had been doing so every hour by now, every day and night.

The first thing I learned at my inaugural commencement as a faculty member was that the gown getup is a lot more involved than the one a graduate wears receiving the diploma. The sleeves come to a sewed-up end, like a straitjacket, and if it weren't for my office mate coming to my rescue, I may have gone the whole event with no use of my hands.

"There are slits for your hands," Jay said as he helped me flip the velvety blue ceremonial hood correctly over my shoulders. That was another detail that surprised me when I opened the gown package. I had no idea how to put it on. "How's your daughter?"

Only a few minutes earlier, I was entirely talkative with Donna about our shared torments, but here, especially today, I hoped not to speak of it at all. Of course, I wanted to acknowledge the kindness of those asking about Anna, as Jay just had, as others had done since the moment I arrived, but without spoiling the festive atmosphere. This was the last day of work, sort of. Everyone in this banquet room being used as a backstage holding area was in the same buzzingly happy state, happy for their students, happy the final grading sprint had ended, happy the months of summer break were here.

"She's okay," I said. "She's going to have the surgery and hopefully—"

"Jesus Christ," Jay said.

"Yeah."

I had only known these colleagues at Mercy for about nine months at this point, and I hadn't met one I didn't like. What I really appreciated was how the few I'd mentioned any of this to didn't try to extend the conversations. It felt to me they were just genuinely troubled for me and only wanted to send the message that I had their support. At our last school faculty meeting, the associate dean gently said to me, "You know, Marc, you don't have to be here right now."

I did feel I had to be there, however, at those meetings, in my classes, and especially there today. This was the kind of job I'd wanted for so long, and I needed it to stay right.

I'd had to get the hell out of my car after Donna and I had hung up, for the fresh air as much as to get to commencement on time. I speed-walked toward the entrance of the convention center, chastising myself for not asking her more questions. I didn't ask the specifics of her son's case, how much brain they'd attempted to remove, or whether it was a lesion like Anna's, or a growing tumor, or multiple areas of tissue from which his seizures came. I knew his surgery wasn't at our hospital, but I wished I'd asked more about the actual procedure. We'd been told by our team that at many other hospitals, this kind of brain surgery was a two-phase process. They'd actually "go in" twice, first to literally poke around and see how the patient responded, in order to tell what area of the brain was working and what was not—a kind of precautionary exploration. Then, they'd close up the wound temporarily and not long after go through the whole thing again, this time actually extracting stuff. Doctor Hoffman's team, though, would be going in only once, doing the exploration and the excision in one shot. This sure felt preferable, not to have Anna under general anesthesia twice, open and close the skull twice, recover from that kind of operation twice, but I had no real understanding of the difference between the approaches in terms of risks and benefits.

In the banquet room, someone holding a camera began calling out for the Liberal Arts School faculty to gather for a photo with the college president. The group of forty or so of us squeezed together in front of the Mercy College background board set up in one of the corners. I stood in the back row, as I usually do for group shots. I thought about how for some ten years as a part timer at City College, especially in the stretches of time when I didn't have a play running somewhere, a commercial on television, or a temporary contract for a stage acting gig, teaching had given me a consistent home base to rely on, a part of my identity that didn't come and go with all my other professional irregularity. Still, as an adjunct, I wasn't part of the department decisions, events, or anything other than my classes. Now, here with these people, in this gown that Dr. Jason Zalinger, PhD had to assist me with, this picture being taken felt like exhibit A in the case of whether I had finally become an official part of some true importance with my work. Of course, I couldn't feel much of a spirit lift out of this observation at the moment, but the first thing I did when the photographer in the room finished the five or six snaps of the group was ask her where I could get one of those photos for myself.

It was time to line up for our processional. I checked my phone. Still nothing from Geri. Most likely, Anna would be on the sofa most of the day, and I knew Geri wouldn't want to contact me unless it was an emergency. When I left, just as she had for the theatre club show, she urged me to try to enjoy myself.

We were lined up in a double line. I stood beside a math professor I'd met once or twice at meetings throughout the school year. Once the organizers began to usher us out of the banquet room and into the center lobby toward the arena doors, everyone became quiet, walking in step with their counterpart in the opposite line. As we moved, I began to hear that famous graduation music, "Pomp and Circumstance." The other sound I could hear, faintly, was all those keys in my pocket.

In my life, I'd made more than my share of self-conscious entrances with audiences watching. All those plays, which could be in front of a hundred; those walks to and from the mound, which could be in front of a thousand; all those first days of class, which could be in front of a couple dozen, knowing how I walked in was the impression that would be the most lasting of all. A bit of nerves was always a companion, but in all those instances, I had a job to do when I got where I was going, a performance to execute, a game to play. Here, I had no other objective but to get to my seat without tripping and thus becoming the long-lasting comic memory of Commencement 2018, the rookie who face-planted on his way to the stage. Maybe, I thought, as the thoughts became louder with every step, I'd stumble ahead, knocking into the person in front of me, setting off a Domino line of faculty dropping forward.

As I successfully sat down in my seat, I figured the exit march would be easier than the entrance, now that I'd done it once. It didn't take long for me to bring Anna into these thoughts, how ironic it was, me in perfect sobriety, stressing out about walking in a line, while she, in the state she was in, was attempting each

evening to join her fellow dancers in executing intricate chore-
ography. I was reminded how fortunate I was that Kristen agreed
to the plan I put forward about sitting out the recital. If Anna
dropped during the dress rehearsal tomorrow, without an audience, it'd be that tree nobody heard in the forest.

I placed my cell phone onto my lap as the provost kicked off
the series of speeches with a warm welcome to the crowd, met
by ecstatic cheers. Still no texts or calls. The valedictorian, the
school deans with the special student awards, the commencement speaker, then the president. No texts or calls. At last, the
main event of the calling of the names, the crossing of the stage,
the handshake, the moment of triumph parents set all sails for
the moment their kid steps into preschool.

I'd tried to ready myself for this part. The obvious, the most
self-abusive thing to do would be to gaze tragically at each and
every new graduate shaking President Timothy Hall's hand, over
the happy hollers of their family members, the flashes from their
cameras, wrestling the temptation to picture Anna there someday, me now a veteran of these ceremonies, never once having
stumbled on the way in, and Kristen somewhere in the audience,
hollering too...the surgery now long ago a success.

I knew that such easy visions would bring a surge of pleasure,
only to be dashed by the quick recollection that in a few weeks,
her skull would be opened, to an end none of us could predict. I
was sure I'd swell with mixed emotion with such imaginings, and
it would be a kind of strange satisfaction just to feel something.
But I fought it.

And so I planned to put my mind to making another list. This
one would be mental and would take my attention away from the
walking graduates and back onto the things scheduled over the
next few weeks, and in what order: the pediatrician clearance,

neuropsych test, blood test, MEG scan, the home instruction, the insurance pre-approvals....

The first few students had crossed the stage when I glanced down at my phone again. A text had come. Not from Geri, but from Anna.

I'M IN THE RECITAL, RIGHT?

This was disorienting at first and made no sense to me. I'd stood beside her days before, carefully laying out our plan, and the very logical reasoning behind it. Reading this text, it was as if Anna hadn't heard a word of what I'd said. I then wondered what occasioned this, right now, from home—had Geri said something? Had Kristen said something? Had it taken this long for her drug-saturated brain to process what I explained? Whatever the case, I had considered this settled business.

YOU'LL DO THE DRESS REHEARSAL

A quick response.

ONLY????

I AM IN THE MIDDLE OF GRADUATION. CALL YOU IN A WHILE

Then, nothing back. I looked up into the lights in the rafters. Students with surnames starting with B were being called through the loudspeaker. I tried to take deep breaths. I was getting angry. With everything we faced, not only the items on that list I meant to make, but all the dreaded rest of it, this recital issue was no longer something I had room for.

I'll explain it again to her, I thought to myself. And that will be that. Exhalation through the mouth.

Another text.

I WORKED SO HARD ON MY DANCES
I KNOW ANNA
I WANT TO BE IN IT

*YOU'LL DO ALL YOUR DANCES TOMORROW AT THE
DRESS IF YOU CAN*
THATS STUPID I WANT TO BE IN THE RECITAL!!!!!!
ANNA I CAN'T DO THIS RIGHT NOW
About a minute later:
I AM IN THE RECITAL
I wanted to stand up and run out. I wanted to call and explode at her. I wanted to throw the phone.
NO YOU ARE NOT, I wrote, then deleted it and wrote nothing. A few minutes passed.
DAD?????
I WILL BE HOME IN A BIT
Before there was time enough to see another text, I shoved the phone in my pants pocket, which took some shifting in my seat, what with the damn gown I was so excited to order in March.

When I got home, Anna was just as I'd left her in the morning. She was on the sofa, watching *The Greatest Showman.* She had her leotard and tights on.

"I don't know how she never gets sick of those songs," I said to Geri. "I got her texts."

"I hadn't said anything. She just started asking me about the recital. Just out of nowhere, she was all upset."

"I told her what the deal was," I said, then looked at Anna on the sofa. "Guess she's moved on now."

"Well, she's been lying down a good hour now. They're dressed for dance, they ate, and Nora even got her homework done."

"Thanks, Geri."

She hugged both girls goodbye and headed out. Anna said nothing to me, and I felt no reason to tempt a continuation of our text dialogue. We had about fifteen minutes before I'd drive

SHE DANCED WITH LIGHTNING

them the few blocks to the dance studio, and I wanted to change into more casual clothes. Nora was sitting near Anna in another chair, drawing in a pad, so I asked her to keep an eye out while I ran upstairs to my room. I wanted to get right back down, so this would be a "quick change," as they put it in the theatre, when an actor leaves a scene only to almost immediately reenter wearing a different costume. Here, I'd change the khakis for gym shorts, the oxford for a t-shirt, and the tall socks and Rockports for a pair of flip-flops. I barely got as far as unbuttoning the oxford.

"Dad!"

Anna pounded on the bedroom door.

"I'm getting changed, Anna."

"You always had chances, Dad!" she yelled. "Chances, chances, chances!"

Such a relaxed state on the sofa moments before, now with fury in her voice behind the door.

"Let me change, Anna. Get your bag and water and be ready to go."

I put my t-shirt on, then started at my belt.

"I want to be in the recital!"

She pounded on the door again.

"Stop it, Anna."

"I want to be in it!"

"Anna, we talked about all of this. You're injured, just like I was, when I had to—"

"It's not the same!" She threw open the door. I was pulling my shorts up. Her eyes were hectic.

"Calm down and breathe. Right now," I said.

"It's not the same! You're not the same as me!"

"Calm down."

"It's not the same because you knew you were gonna live! You knew you'd be alive after!"

I took a beat to deescalate. That was a zinger she'd delivered, for sure, a scene-topper of a line. I let some air in, then spoke calmly.

"Anna, you're not going to die," I said. "You heard the doctor."

"I don't care if I do," she said. Her voice then went from restrained to booming and savage: "I can't sleep or talk! Or think or walk or see! So I'll die, and it'll be over!"

"They're going to make everything better, that's why we—"

"I love dancing, and you won't let me!"

"I am letting you go to class, Anna. Right? Now let's go to class."

She came at me, grabbing the shirt I'd just put on and pulled so hard that the cotton crew collar tore and burned the back of my neck. I grabbed her hands, pulled them off me, and pushed her to my arms' length. I slid my hands up to her elbows and put my face into hers. We were nearly nose to nose, my eyes in hers as they blinked, dilated, and spun.

"You listen to me, goddamnit. There's a storm in your head, Anna. It's raging. Right now. I can see it in your eyes. Lightning. It'll start there in your eyes, then it'll be in your arms, then your legs, and if we stand here, like this, and I let you go, you'll fall like a ragdoll. You cannot be in a show right now, Anna. That is not what's important right now. You're not making sense. You go out there on stage like this, start to dance in front of that audience, all those people, with all your friends who have worked just as hard as you have, and out of nowhere, something will explode inside you, and you will go down."

"You...you can't st...stop me!" she wiggled and leaned back.

"I'm your father, Anna. This is what parents have to do," I took one hand off her and pointed at the window. "If there was thunder outside, wind blowing trees down, lightning ripping up the ground, you think I'd let you out there to dance in it?"

She leaned back in. Her face fell back onto mine. Her skin was drenched. She opened her mouth as if to shout, but she stopped herself.

"I'd dance *with* it if it was my last chance," she then said, suddenly with composure. "I'd take it like a partner and dance until it burned me up."

"Anna," I said.

She pushed away again. Before I got my hand back on her, Nora yelled from downstairs that we were going to be late. Anna twisted out of my grip, turned her back, and stomped off down the hall toward the stairs. I threw open my closet to grab my flip-flops when I heard Nora again.

"Daddy! Hurry! Hurry! Anna!"

My right bare foot smacked hard against the closet door as I scrambled, slipping toward the bedroom door and down the hall. There, on the second step from the top, was Nora, holding Anna with all her might.

"She's having a seizure!" Nora was screaming. "I can't hold on!"

I got to them and swung my arm across Anna's hips. Nora fell back onto the top step. I walked Anna, who was shaking hard, legs locked, slowly down the tall wooden staircase to the living room landing.

"N...Nora...Nora...saved me," Anna was mumbling. "I...I... love m...my sister..."

"That's right, Anna. That's right. I've got you."

As I got her to the sofa, I reached to adjust a pillow, clearing a space on which to lay her down. Under my other arm, I felt her violently wriggle away. She stumbled sideways, hit the living room wall, then reached for the front doorknob. Before I could grab her, she made it outside. I followed as Nora yelled her name from the top of the stairs.

Anna made it the few steps down our cement path that led to the sidewalk of the street, made a hard left as if to run off, then froze. She leaned, then, sagging to her right side, slowly at first, dropped, hard, to the ground. Her body hit the asphalt, her head hit grass. There were kids on scooters looking on, neighbors we didn't know very well, who were standing some distance away, covering their mouths.

I ran to her. She was looking at the sky. I slipped my arms under her neck and back, and pried her off the ground, lifting her toward me.

"It's okay, sweetheart," I said. "I have you. It's okay."

"Nora...." she mumbled, closing her eyes. Saliva bubbled off her bottom lip.

"It's Daddy, honey," I said.

"Nora, I fell down," she continued. "I think I had a seizure."

"It's me, baby. It's Daddy. I've got you."

"Please don't tell Daddy," Anna said, opening her eyes, looking right at me. "Please, Nora. Please don't tell him. Don't tell Daddy I had a seizure."

CHAPTER THIRTEEN

WAITING

The following day, Kristen brought the girls to the dress rehearsal at the nearby Queens Performing Arts Center on the campus of Queensborough Community College. I did my best to avoid displaying my concern to Anna as I assisted in making sure their bags were packed with all the different shoes, tights, water bottles, and snacks. I was tiptoeing now. After the scene the day before, the last thing I wanted to do was ruffle feathers. If it were up to me, I'd have her shut down on the sofa, but this had been the agreement. They'd go.

Once they left, the house was in a quiet I could hardly recognize. I made my way to the master bedroom and dropped on the bed. Rosalind curled up at my feet, the spot she usually took with Kristen. Not only had this dog failed to ever become a seizure-detecting heroine, she never snuggled either. For the first time in I didn't know how long, I slept.

When I woke up, I called Kristen, who answered from a diner parking lot, waiting for an order to be ready for pickup. It was nearly 9 p.m.

"The diner?" I said. "On your own volition? Things really have changed."

"It's Anna's meal," she said. "Nora and I picked up sushi first. Want anything?"

She told me that she'd sat with Anna in the auditorium for a good part of the rehearsal, watching the dances. I could hardly envision it, but Anna did manage to get through a few of the numbers without incident. Kristen described how whenever Anna was on stage, she and Annmarie hid behind a flat tucked into the wings, one stage right, one stage left, ready to snatch her. Anna got quickly winded as her dances began, but made it through.

In the auditorium seats, seated beside Kristen as she took video of Nora dancing, Anna had a few of the kind of seizures we'd been seeing recently. They'd hit her without warning, strangle her breath for a few moments, shake her arms, stiffen her legs, then release. Kristen held her until they were over.

"If that had happened on the stage," I began.

"Yeah," Kristen said. "But they didn't."

I was elated the rehearsal was finally past, even feeling a sense of accomplishment for all of us. She'd gotten up there for those few dances in this broken condition. The timing of the seizures was pure luck. Nobody noticed them but Kristen, and nothing of the others' work was disturbed. As we spoke, I could hear the girls' voices in the backseat, unclear as to what they were saying. What was clear, though, was that they were happy.

We had a month to surgery, but over the following week, Anna embarked on a kind of short farewell tour. The day after the dress rehearsal, I brought Anna with me when picking Nora up from the regular Friday Girl Scouts meeting, which met at the local elementary school. I didn't know they had planned it, but they had cards for her and a stuffed fuzzy bear, which, when squeezed, uttered a tinny "Feel better, Anna. We love you!" in the recorded voice of the den mother's youngest daughter.

Knowing she wouldn't be returning to school for the rest of year, the guidance office at the middle school put together a gift basket with another stuffed animal and a large, ornate card with notes of well-wishes from Anna's classmates and teachers. We arranged a brief stop-in to pick it up one midweek morning. We were met by Mrs. Kelly, the school nurse, and some of the guidance counselors. To my surprise, Anna insisted on showing up at whatever class was in session at the moment ("library"), and with my approval on the condition that this surprise appearance lasted no longer than five minutes, we walked Anna down the hall.

As I stood by her, she hugged each classmate, saying thanks for the card and that she missed them. Anna had encountered the typical range of personalities during her first middle school year, from the warm, the stoic, the unpredictable, to the downright bully. This morning, all of them went in for the hug like Anna was a bosom buddy. Ms. Lee was there too. She hugged her the longest, in the classroom then again in the lobby, and in her thick Korean accent, wished God's blessings on her.

Loving gestures came from many directions. My department at Mercy sent a basket of fancy cookies. The mother of one of the students I would pick up for school in the morning, who assumed my driver role once Anna was out, brought over exquisite home-cooked dishes. Kristen's siblings all pitched in to have meals sent that filled our freezer to capacity. My siblings' kids and Anna's cousins on Kristen's side would text and FaceTime her.

Meanwhile, Kristen dragged herself to work each morning, saving any personal absence days for the surgery and hospitalization ahead. I was rarely more than a few feet from Anna at all times, save the three hours my mother stayed with her as I went into Manhattan to pick up a CD of previous scans and EEG information from NYU, where all her previous doctors hurried to get us anything useful they could provide the surgeons.

Most of the day I plugged away at more phone calls to make our appointments and the forms each specialist required: surveys of Anna's birth history, social information, developmental data, allergies, nutrition, skeletal and muscular systems, and so on. After being on hold for fifty minutes, I resolved the Cohen's private room bill with an affable customer service rep, who canceled it with one keystroke and wished Anna a swift recovery.

The home instructor from the school district came later in the week for an introductory visit, explaining how the few-hour sessions would work leading up to the surgery week. I was relieved to find her entirely sympathetic, a young parent herself, who made it clear she was not expecting Anna to be capable of much other than very basic academic exercises in her current state.

The seizures continued, day and night, large and small. I saw no reason she should continue with this final week of dance classes. I felt it would only be painful for Anna to return to the studio while, obvious to me, the imminent recital would be on everyone's mind. On top of that, the theatre director in me assumed that a week without Anna would help the teachers adjust the dances to accommodate her absence from the final performance.

She hadn't brought the recital up since the rehearsal, nor had I. After the dress rehearsal, I assumed she had finally come to see things as I did, that a regretful but realistic decision to miss the show was her only choice. The only question now was whether she would want to attend as a spectator, to see her sister and her friends on stage. If she did, my plan was to seat the two of us deep in the back of the auditorium, near a door, and if a seizure came that grew beyond the kind nobody would notice, I'd move us swiftly into the hall.

If Anna would be too delirious that morning and didn't want to go, I had another plan. Kristen would go with Nora, and I'd call in for a delivery of breakfast from the diner. As there were two performances, an earlier morning show and another in the afternoon, Kristen and I could switch places between them, allowing us both to be there for Nora. These determinations, none of which I had yet discussed with Kristen, had satisfied me completely.

Friday evening, the night before the recital, I walked Anna upstairs to the bathroom. She got herself into the shallow bath water, and I sat on the floor outside the tub. As either Kristen or I would always do as she bathed, I'd keep her talking the entire time behind the curtain, to ensure she hadn't seized and gone under. We were discussing the importance of thoroughly rinsing the shampoo out of her hair, when I caught a glimpse of both dance costume bags being rolled down the hall: Nora's *and* Anna's. Unnerved though I was, I waited until both girls were asleep before confronting Kristen.

"What are you doing?" I said to Kristen. We were in the living room. The bags were on the floor, packed and zipped. Anna was asleep in the sofa.

How this came out of my mouth surprised me. In the two hours or so waiting for both girls to go to bed, silently incensed with my wife, I expected an instant verbal melee, played out in stage whisper, because Anna was right there. But I launched the first salvo with this question already feeling defeated. My voice was no more charged with emotion than if I were asking her the same question just to start any old conversation.

"What's up with Anna's bag here?"

"Anna wants to try to do the recital. Everyone there will be ready," Kristen said.

"She can't."

"I talked to Annmarie. Everyone wants her to do what she feels she can."

"You will regret this. You are consciously, in sound body and mind, both of which Anna is not, waltzing into a huge mistake."

"I talked to Anna, and she—"

"Talked to Anna? When? And why was I not involved?"

"Well, we know your position on this."

"Oh, that sets a healthy precedent," I hissed, louder. "If Dad has a contrary opinion to what the eleven-year-old thinks, let's leave him out of the conversation!"

"All the teachers will be in the wings. I will be too."

"You think teachers grabbing a seizing dancer in the middle of a performance will be any less traumatizing to everyone there? Have you thought about the other kids and what they'll go through? Nora included?"

"Anna said if she starts feeling anything, she'll skip off stage, just like she does in class."

"Skip off stage? They haven't been coming with a warning, Kristen. Last week, she hit the pavement like she got shot!"

"I'm confident we will deal with it."

"I'm out!" I said. Full-voiced. "No way. That's it. I will not...I won't subject myself to it."

"What do you mean? You won't go?"

"No way."

"Are you serious?" Kristen said.

"Absolutely," I continued, quieter. "I can't. I won't. Nobody with any sense would do this. I'm out. It's wrong."

Anna's soft voice came from behind me.

"What's wrong?" she said.

"Anna, go to sleep," I said, turning around.

"What did you say?" she said, looking at me.

"I'm talking to Mom—"

"About tomorrow," Anna cut me off.

"Yes. And I'm sorry. I...can't. I just found out I can't go. I can't see the recital."

"Why not?"

"I have to..." Looking at her there, her eyes attentive and expectant back into mine, I could see tomorrow. I could see those eyes. From the stage. Her eyes, finding me on the aisle in the dark, just as the bolt fires inside her. Here again, that look of hers so many years ago, a toddler dancing on the table, falling, just within my reach. I could see myself tomorrow, in my seat, breathless, lungs as if yanked out of me from below. I saw her fumbling a step, then dropping forward, the audience in a gasp that overcomes the music. I saw her groping, clawing at the shiny black dance floor. The music would play on, the dancers scattered about, some continuing the routine unawares, others frozen in shock, others somewhere in between. And all the while, Anna's eyes would be on me.

"I have to work," I said.

Anna, without expression, rolled to her right, and went back to sleep. Kristen said she'd stay beside her tonight on the floor. I'd sleep in the bedroom, I told her. I'd close the door and sleep as late as I could. As if things could get even more grotesque, she told me that she'd offered some of the extra tickets we'd bought to my brother Scott and his family, and they were coming from Rhode Island to join my parents to see the second performance.

"Good luck," I said. "I'll be here at home. And please, I don't want details. Ever."

The next morning, I was up early but didn't leave the room. Through the closed door, the raucous corralling of the girls to be ready and out sounded no different than on any recital morning of the past. I lay there expecting Kristen to come through the bedroom door in surrender to what she figured I'd find good news: that Anna had however many seizures through the night and morning, and had gone back to sleep on the sofa. But all at once, the ruckus stopped, the front door slammed closed, and Kristen's car pulled away.

My first move was to check the pill organizer to confirm Anna had taken the morning share of medicine. She had. I showered, dressed, walked to the Wan Wan Mart for coffee, came back, and sat in our small backyard with Rosalind at my feet. I thought I'd try to read but couldn't. I thought I'd try to write in my journal, but I couldn't. I thought I'd make that list of things left to do in the three weeks to surgery but couldn't. With my large deli-cup coffee, now nearly empty in one hand, my phone in the other, I just sat there until it was curtain time for the first performance just a few short miles away.

I could see right off that this boycott of sorts might not be much easier than actually sitting in the auditorium watching. In my restlessness I sent a text to Kristen, telling her that when something happened and Anna needed picking up, I'd speed over so that she could stay to watch Nora.

The longer I waited for Kristen to text me back, the more tense I felt. After a few minutes, I wanted to text again, or call, but I resisted. As I paced around the little yard, four people who had left this Earth years before came to mind, all of whose blood was running through Anna at this very moment. My grandparents.

Years ago, I was interviewing my mother's father, Edward Gaffney, researching a play I was writing. He had earned a Bronze Star Medal and Purple Heart as a Staff Sergeant in the 4th Infantry Division in World War II. One day, in 1945, as the US and Red Army closed in on Berlin, his company was shelled in the Harz Mountains. My grandmother Mae received a telegram from the Secretary of War that her new husband was missing in action, then another days later, informing her that he was seriously wounded. As she sat there day after day awaiting the next telegram, Edward woke up in a field hospital in France, was told about the shrapnel that had entered his legs, and that everyone around him had been killed in the attack.

In all of this, what he said was the worst thing he remembered about war was the waiting. He told me he really didn't remember much about the moment of the explosion...a sound, the pain, the heat...but most of what he recalled were the days, weeks, months of waiting for something like that shelling to happen to him and his men. Every minute, every second, could come the end.

"There's nothing like the waiting," he said. My grandmother agreed.

Forty minutes past showtime. Nothing on my phone.

I thought of Edmund Palmieri, who was turned down by the Army for flat feet, while his three brothers went to fight in Europe. Nonetheless, he too did his tour of warrish waiting when his first child, who would be my father, caught the whooping cough in 1947. They called it "The 100 Day Cough" back then, and while most survived the 150,000 something cases that year, for babies, it was highly deadly. The doctor informed the parents that the case would likely steadily worsen toward a dangerous crisis, and if that crisis could be survived, there'd be hope. For weeks, infant Frank hacked and coughed out the atrocious sound of late-stage pertussis, and my grandmother, as directed, held him in an upright position through the sleepless nights. By day, Edmund worked extra jobs beyond his factory shifts, like sweeping the stoops of Elizabeth, New Jersey, then sold the car he drove to work, in order to buy rabbit serum, a treatment purported to help. One morning, my father came to the tipping point. He stopped coughing and turned blue. My great grandfather George, a brakeman on the railroads, who happened to be in the house, came running and gave CPR. A breath punched out, the lungs expanded, and the unlikely recovery had begun.

They were all gone now, my grandparents, but I wished I could talk to them. I wished I could ask them if I'd ever done anything right.

I texted Kristen again. From what I could estimate, by now the show should nearly be over.

SHE DID FIVE DANCES, Kristen texted back.

WOW, I wrote.

NO SEIZURES

I dropped the coffee cup, ripped open the back door and grabbed my car keys. I texted while I drove.

IS IT ALMOST OVER, I wrote.

YES. SITTING OUT THE LAST BALLET TO REST

I was about to write that this was it, she had done it. She had gotten through. A miracle. But it was too much to text as I was moving so fast up Springfield Boulevard. I'd already nearly rear-ended the same van twice. Another text came.

SHE WANTS TO SAVE HER ENERGY, Kristen wrote.

THE SECOND SHOW? I wrote.

YES

I wanted to say no again, please no, that's too much. Cut and run now. Enough is enough. She's had enough. Then, another text.

YOU HAVE TO BE HERE

Kristen had left my ticket with my brother Scott, whom I met in front of the performance center. He and his family had arrived the night before and stayed with my parents on Long Island. They were all there too, already in their seats for the second show. Kristen hung back with Anna in the dressing room areas, where the hundred or so dancers ate something and prepared themselves for a second marathon in controlled mayhem of entrances, exits and costume changes. All the studio age groups took part in these recitals, and parents like Kristen were heavily relied upon to help keep order backstage. I didn't bother attempting to go back there, to congratulate Anna on doing what she did and maybe, in the felicity of it all, encourage her to quit while she was ahead. I wanted to, but I knew I had no chance.

Scott and I didn't talk much as we got in line to enter. I didn't have much to say other than that I feared we were in for the most terrifying dance recital in human history. I looked around at the faces of parents, grandparents, aunts, uncles, siblings, and friends and thought how they were so happily ignorant of the possible drama included with today's twenty-dollar ticket, that the tall, blonde, beautiful, eye-grabbing sixth grader may very well collapse in dramatic fashion while they looked on in adoration at their own dancing loved one.

"This is a bizarre moment," I said to my brother as the lines were fully formed, stretched from the lobby outside into the campus quad. "I'm lined up to go in there and suffer. Actually moving forward in an orderly fashion, to willingly sit there and agonize for two hours, on the edge of my seat, totally incapable of doing anything if something happens."

"She'll be okay," he said, surely wishing I hadn't spoken at all. I wondered why he was putting himself through this and not running for his car.

"It's like I'm a Christian at the Roman Colosseum come to see my kid against the lions," I kept on. "Great seats, but do I really want them?"

We filed in. I asked Scott to sit with me as far back as we could get, where there were a few stretches of half-empty rows. The further back, the darker it would be in the house, away from the reflection of the stage lights, and the fewer faces I could see in the audience. I looked over the playbill, which listed the order of the thirty-something acts to come, by title of song and cast. Anna and Nora were in eight of them, spread well apart across the list.

I tried to think of this being over with, in the car on the way home, back to the living room, Anna on the sofa, *The Greatest Showman* on the television. However terrible this imminent moment might be, I tried to think, it will, after all, come and go. If she wanted, if she was ever healthy enough to dance again, she could change studios, start again somewhere else. There were other studios in Queens.

Anna would be in the very first act, which was a big, full company tap and jazz piece from the show *Hairspray*. The curtain time arrived, but the lights in the house stayed on for another ten minutes. This wasn't uncommon at these things. They would hold the curtain for as long as they reasonably could for the people who were still pouring into the auditorium to find their seats. I fought off the thought that the delay was caused by Anna backstage in a seizure, Kristen tending to her, and the others taking this borrowed time to recover from the upset of it all.

Darkness. Music. The theatrical lights blasted the stage, and on came the dancers. The whole company in a full, bouncing trot. There was Nora, and there was Anna. I was bobbing my legs. I made both hands into fists, pushed myself back into the folding auditorium seat, squirming, shrinking, wishing I could look away. I watched only Anna's face at first, her smiling, glittering face, looking for that strike, that pop of a change in expression, when all would turn from this razzle dazzle beaming bliss to terror.

Everyone in step, in line, not a hint of imbalance or distraction. The stage only movement, lines of an aqua-colored blur, the lustrous bodies flowing, wheeling past, carrying Anna's face. The button on the song, blackout, silence, hollers, and applause. One down. I exhaled. Stage lights went up to half, the auditorium quieted again as a young teacher led a string of what look like toddlers in bumble bee costumes to center stage. Voluble sighs and loving chuckles rolled across the crowd. My brother gently touched my arm.

"She was perfect," Scott said. "They both were."

He moved to light the playbill with his phone to see how long we had before Anna's next appearance.

"Three more and they're on again," I said.

"What, did you memorize this?"

"I think I might have," I said.

The time between my daughters' appearances felt incomparably shorter than in years past. The gap of performances by the other groups and classes could be up to five dances long, normally bringing a daunting challenge to avoid nodding off. Not the case this time. The fraught in between passed all too quickly. I spent each interval relieved at Anna's getting through the prior dance, only to wonder in high anxiety if, when we got to her next, the cast would enter, and she wouldn't be there.

Each time, though, with a quiet, "Here we go," muttered to my brother beside me, Anna came on, again. Then again, and again, with no discernable problem, even under the acute and crazed scrutiny of her father's long-distance vision. As the show progressed, I found my eyes daring to drift off her face, and, in marvel, at her legs and feet nailing her turns, landing her leaps, staying in perfect cadence with the rest. These legs and feet, so strong and solid, that weeks ago folded under her as she tried to walk from the hospital bed to the bathroom. In the middle of a duet with Kalli's daughter Andrea, to "Anything You Can Do (I Can Do Better)," Anna suddenly stopped, pivoted a three-quarter turn to face downstage, threw her hands in the air, and did a perfect cartwheel. Blackout. A roar of hoots, clapping, and whistles. Then, the company finale. Curtain call. My brother's hand again on my arm, this time firm.

Outside on the cobblestone quad, in a small, cheerful sea of people, Anna and Nora stood in the last costume they'd worn in the show. They were arm in arm, holding the flowers their grandparents had given them, smiling for pictures. Fellow dancers came and went for group shots and hugs of celebration. It would be the only one of the sixty-eight days between that April morning on the softball field and her surgery in June, on which Anna would not have a seizure.

It was a scene of triumph, the prize of nearly a year of all their work, and the hour of fulfilment for Anna that I had done by best to deny. And it was also a scene Aristotle would call one of *anagnorisis*. The recognition scene. The moment in the play where a man moves from blindness to full, merciless comprehension of who he is, or who he ain't. In fine poetic form here, too, so close to the end of the story.

The man, of course, is me, midway through his degraded life of chasing dream upon dream but for the grace of his unearned privilege of infinite chances. I had been one who tried and tried to at last become somebody I might finally respect. What possible place did I have, in perfect health, to stand in her way, as she, facing an unknowable, unthinkable tomorrow, demanded this one chance to do the thing that made her punished life most livable? Who on Earth but her could say what is best, what is right, what ought to be enough for her, my disabled child? Who?

If it's anyone at all, it ain't me.

We walked in silence to our car in the parking lot. I held Nora's hand. In front of me was Anna, her hand in Kristen's. I wasn't sure what to say, what should be said, and what shouldn't. I wanted to say aloud that I had been wrong, Anna, that I knew it now and that I was glad, so glad, that you defied me. I wanted to say that I had been afraid of so much, that I still was, and would always be. I wanted to say that here, though, in the midst of this dreadful season, it was a happy day indeed, for all of us, because the dance was beautiful and that you, my daughter, pitted from birth in a war for your life, are stronger than your father.

"Best recital yet," I finally said. "Both of you were amazing. How do you feel?"

"Good!" Nora cheered.

"Good," Anna said. "I can't believe it's over. I'm sad it's over."

"All that work, and it's over," Nora added. "I'm sad too."

"Well, that's a good kind of sad," I said.

"A good kind of sad?" said Anna.

"Yes. It's a sad you only have when you love something so much."

We got to the car. We would get food at a restaurant near the house.

"It all starts again in the fall," Kristen said. "Then, a year from now, another show."

I said that was right. Absolutely right. Next year there'd be another show and we would be here, right here. All of us, again.

I wanted to, and I tried, all the way to the restaurant, all the way home, all the way to June 18, to believe it.

CHAPTER FOURTEEN

GOODBYE

W e were "scrubbed," standing in a kind of hermetic wind chamber in our thin paper hospital gowns before we were walked along the slow-rolling bed toward the operating room. The double doors opened onto something like the control room of Starship Enterprise. Spaceship lighting; computer monitors facing all directions tilted at viewing angles from the ceiling and on rolling stands; laptops and long trays of blunt and bladed instruments that ranged from things I'd see in a drawer at the periodontists' office to things I'd expect to see on a medieval battlefield. Nurses, technicians, and other specialty doctors like anesthesiologists and reconstructive surgeons worked busily with their keyboards. I saw Dr. Hoffman through a small window in a door to another room on a phone. She looked up at me, then looked away.

There was a magic marker "X" drawn on the left side of Anna's neck. Back in my periodontist typing days, I'd heard tell of molars being extracted on the wrong side of the mouth, so I supposed even here something like that was possible, so X marked the left frontal lobe.

Anna was crying and had been for a good hour. Her fear was coming to its height now, naturally, but it was hunger that hurt the most. In prep for the general anesthetic, she hadn't been allowed to eat anything since early the night before, and we were now into early afternoon. It reminded me of the first visit we had with her here, in her mother's arms, waiting for brain scans, crying because she couldn't eat.

A kind of emotional shutdown was over both Kristen and me as they lifted Anna from the bed onto the operating table, fitting her head in a padded securing vice. A technician, in an urgent but tender Spanish accent, told us that it was time to say goodbye, that she'd soon be put under, and as soon as her eyes closed, we needed to quickly exit.

"See you soon, Anna," I said, forcing a smile. "I love you so much."

"I'm scared," she said.

"I know. It's almost over."

"I love you, my sweet, beautiful baby," Kristen said. "We will be right outside."

The mask was placed over the nose and mouth, and after a breath, she was out.

"Mom, Dad, you must follow me now," said the tech.

There was a waiting area for families off the main hall of the neurosurgery floor, near the reception area. Our group, made up of Anna's grandparents, our siblings, and friends, took up a significant area. I did my best to stay there as long as I could, feeling somewhat responsible for this, like I was hosting a white-knuckled cocktail party. My father ran for sandwiches on First Avenue. We were in for hours of waiting.

I wandered from time to time out of the area and onto a bench in the hall, where there was total quiet solitude, visited here and there by my sister Kaitlin, who was a comfort to me in understanding this kind of hospital surreality. She was no stranger to it, having lost a loved one in an accident not two years earlier, a man who hung on for some days in an ICU. I told her I felt better here in the hall, peering intermittently in the direction from which I knew that at some point, a doctor, surgeon, or social worker would come up the hall with news. I wanted to be there and hear it first, whatever it was, alone.

I got a text from Randy. She told me she was downstairs in the hospital lobby and asked if I wanted her to come up. Kait suggested I head down for some air and to see my friend.

We sat on one of the sofas in the entrance area.

"I can't believe that right now, at this moment, her skull is sawed open."

"Want some booze? A pill?" Randy said.

"I'd probably just puke and crash right here and get thrown to the curb."

She turned and looked at a plaque listing hospital donors on the wall behind us. One of the names was her father, Peter Jay Sharp.

"My father," she said. "There he is."

Once a master of the city. Owner of the Carlisle Hotel, patron of the arts, a legend of a rags to riches life. He died of cancer when Randy was in her twenties. Randy, despite her accomplishments in the theatre, spoke often about not living up to his successes. There were different details, but we often agreed we shared a similar story: we wanted much more from ourselves and hadn't found it.

"All along, I've said to you. Think about what this could mean for Anna. Not what could go wrong, but how she could be free of this. How you and Kristen could be free of this. Imagine that, Marc?"

"I can't," I said. "I've tried, but I can't. The only thing I want right now is for her to survive this operation."

We hung out there a while, and I was more than grateful for the time it burned. Nearly an hour now. Randy handed me a small bag with protein bars and a small airport bottle of liquor.

"I love you," she said. "And you both done right by that kid."

I went back through security and to the elevator upstairs.

Back on the bench, I continued to keep the hallway in my peripheral vision. More family and friends arrived as the hours passed. There was my Bayside friend Chuck who worked in midtown and hadn't been in this hospital since his daughter, now one of Anna's best friends, was born dangerously premature.

"It's like yesterday," he said. "When we were here with Victoria. It all came back the second I stepped inside."

For weeks, I had thought about what life might be, what anything would mean, if Anna was gone, or if after this, what I knew of her was now no more, if the seizures still came, if uncontrollable bleeding, infection, or a stroke ensued. None of it was possible to think of now, nor was anything Randy urged me to consider. My mind had only pure awareness of time, in helpless waiting.

Then, there was Dr. Nangia, walking briskly down the hall. She was looking at her phone, with an expression that I immediately judged meant Anna was alive. She saw me and smiled.

"She'd doing great," she said, smiling wide. "They're taking the lesion out now."

All that time must have been the explorative part, I thought. The opening of the head and testing the brain's areas for what worked and what didn't.

"Nothing went wrong?" I said.

"No, no. She's great! The lesion will come out, the gap will fill with fluid for a few days, and then, over time, we'll see what the outcome is. They think they got it all. Look, I will tell you, I've seen patients seize the very next day, you have to be prepared, and of course we've seen them never seize again. We are very optimistic, but it's possible that some network in the brain is left that can put her at risk. But so far, things look good."

She went in to tell the group in the waiting area. I followed. Hugs all around. I was breathing normally. I'm not sure I considered in all my wondering the possibility that we'd see the end of epilepsy. That seemed too much to ask. I knew that she was alive. That was enough. From here, there was life, and we would live it with her.

Dr. Schwartz came in soon after, at ease and jovial, happy to report the same. To everyone's laughter he said he, too, wanted hugs. From everyone there. Dr. Hoffman followed a few minutes later. The lesion was out, she told us. It was about the size of a cork. They were now reconstructing the skull.

"Dr. Hoffman," Geri said. "We understand there's no way to know if seizures could come back."

"We believe we got it," she said. "Theoretically, it's all over."

In a few hours, Anna was asleep in the PICU. A perfectly fitted white gauze cap covered her head from forehead to nape, with two long blonde pigtails shooting out of two slits. Beside her on her pillow was placed a small stuffed puppy, wearing an identical gauze cap, ears shooting out like the pigtails.

Days of monitoring, MRIs, clinical tests, her ankles and face swelling with bruises and black eyes. Everything had gone as we'd been told it would. On day six, she was discharged, rolled out to our car in a wheelchair, and brought home. The medicine would be weaned slowly, across a year's time. The visiting teacher resumed visits. Anna passed sixth grade. Summer began, and soon it was Happy Fourth in Rhode Island. The first med completely shed was the strongest, the Levetiracetam. No seizures.

In a few weeks, I called Rich in Florida to give the update. By late fall, the second med, Lacosamide, was weaned. Her face's swelling had reduced almost to normal. She had returned to dance and made honor roll for the first marking period of seventh grade.

About eight months after the surgery, on the way to a night class, I called Donna. She said her son was doing well. He was approaching a year of seizure freedom, and making headway in his campaign for a car.

"If only this could be it," she said. "For both of them. If only. Please, God."

"If only," I agreed. "Thank you, Donna."

A few weeks later, the hospital wrote telling us that the *Daily News* was interested in doing an article about Anna.

Over three years seizure free, Anna plays varsity soccer at the Queens High School of Teaching, and is a company member with her sister at the beautiful and thriving Annmarie's Studio of Performing Arts a few miles from us in Great Neck. They both dream of attending Mercy College and dorming there. Nora hasn't had a stomachache in as long as we can remember.

In all of this, this divine normal, no one can say that Anna's epilepsy is a thing we've seen the last of. The brain is a mystery, a contraption of wires and sparks, ever changing through a human life. In these years since the surgery, we've heard of so many stories like that of Cameron Boyce. There was nine-year-old Sophia in our very neighborhood who one morning died of SUDEP. There was the teenage gymnast in nearby Whitestone who had a grand mal an hour before a meet. A stranger walking past me on 8th Avenue in Manhattan to meet friends, brought down by the epileptic's sniper, ever lying in ambush, leaving him concussed in the back of his skull.

"Did I fall down?" he said to me as he stopped shaking and came to. I was kneeling at his side, his bleeding head in my hands. The ambulance I called was on its way.

"Yes," I said. "Your backpack helped break the fall."

"That's why I wear one," he said. Then, after a silence, "A helmet is too embarrassing. But I thought I was done with this. It's been so long. God almighty. Why?"

I no longer spend my nights on the floor. Often, it's been the living room sofa. It sits against a wall directly beneath Anna's room. If she fell, I'd be sure to hear the impact from below.

Recently, though, I've begun to make it through nights beside my wife in our bed. I kiss both girls goodnight in their bedrooms, then walk down the hall into our own. I turn off the lights, lie down, and slow my heart with the deep breathing we once learned together from the social worker's pamphlets. Slowly I'm lulled from that certain alarm I know will attend me the rest of my life as a parent and into a delicate, reluctant sleep.

ABOUT THE AUTHOR

Author photo by John Painz

M arc Palmieri is a playwright, actor, screenwriter, baseball coach, and college professor. His plays include *Waiting For the Host*, *The Groundling*, *Carl the Second*, and the *New York Times*'s "Critic's Pick" *Levittown* (all published by Dramatists Play Service, Inc.). His screenplays include Miramax's *Telling You* (1999). He has published short fiction in *Fiction*, and short memoir in *Global City Review* and *(Re) An Ideas Journal*. Marc has appeared in many national television commercials, soap operas, and stage productions. He played baseball for Wake Forest University and was drafted by the Toronto Blue Jays, and continues to coach at the high school level. Marc is an assistant professor at Mercy College's School of Liberal Arts in Dobbs Ferry, New York. He has also taught for a decade at The City College of New York's MFA program in creative writing. Marc lives in New York City.